Complete
MASONRY

By Steve Cory and the Editors of Sunset Books, Menlo Park, California

SAFETY Sunset Publishing Corporation cannot be held responsible for adapting the ideas, plans or designs in this book to local site conditions, design changes or construction means or methods utilized in construction. The publisher makes no warranties of any kind, express or implied, regarding the construction and use of any of those ideas, plans, or designs and will not be liable for any injuries incurred during the construction and/or use of those ideas, plans, or designs.

SUNSET BOOKS

VICE PRESIDENT AND GENERAL MANAGER: Richard A. Smeby
VICE PRESIDENT AND EDITORIAL DIRECTOR: Bob Doyle
PRODUCTION DIRECTOR: Lory Day
OPERATIONS DIRECTOR: Rosann Sutherland
RETAIL SALES DEVELOPMENT MANAGER: Linda Barker
EXECUTIVE EDITOR: Bridget Biscotti Bradley
ART DIRECTOR: Vasken Guiragossian

STAFF FOR THIS BOOK
Writer: Steve Cory
Contributing Editor: Mara Wildfeuer
Photo Stylist and Builder: Ryan Fortini
Principal Photographer: Frank Gaglione
Illustrator: Bill Oetinger
Photo Editor: Jane Martin
Prepress Coordinator: Danielle Javier
Special Contributor: Carrie Dodson
Proofreader: David Sweet
Indexer: Nanette Cardon

EDITING AND LAYOUT BY
NAILHAUS PUBLICATIONS, INC.
Publishing Director: David Schiff
Art Director: Annie Jeon
Copyeditor: Eloisa Pope, PhD.

Cover: Photograph by Thomas J. Story. Quarrystone Custom Blend concrete pavers by Calstone; California Gold slate entry stair risers by Alpha Granite and Marble; Chocolate flagstone entry stair treads by Peninsula Building Materials.

10 9 8 7 6 5 4 3 2
First printing January 2004
Copyright 2004 Sunset Publishing Corporation,
Menlo Park, CA 94025.
Library of Congress Catalog Card Number: 2003110993
ISBN 0-376-01595-0
Printed in the United States

For additional copies of *Complete Masonry* or any other Sunset book, call 1-800-526-5111 or visit us at www.sunset.com.

contents

planning outdoor spaces

WHEN DESIGNING YOUR OUTDOOR LIVING SPACE, START BY considering the many possibilities; you can always narrow down your ideas later. Even if you can't do all the work this year, come up with a complete plan, which may include patios areas, paths, walls, raised beds, and, perhaps, a structure such as an outdoor kitchen counter. ■ In order to examine a broad range of design ideas, this chapter begins with a photo gallery, followed by an overview of the design process. On pages 20–27, you'll see how other homeowners have designed masonry structures to suit various types of yards. Pages 28–35 describe the building materials to help you decide which are best for your situation. Pages 36–39 show how to organize your design ideas and material choices into a solid plan, complete with drawings. Pages 40–43 show two landscaping options that harmonize with masonry projects—a rock garden and crevice plants. The last pages of the chapter describe the tools you'll need.

layouts that work

An outdoor setting should not only look great, it should also suit your life. A good layout avoids bottlenecks and offers ample space for common activities. Gardening, dining, cooking, and entertaining will all be more pleasant with the right layout, and a well-situated lounge area will be a welcome retreat at the end of the day. A functional layout is often an attractive layout, because it exudes a comfortable, lived-in ambience.

▲ FOR LOUNGING OR DINING

This patio gives a comfortably spacious feel for two lounge chairs, but it's also ready for the occasional cookout. A V-shaped flower bed subtly divides the patio in two; the smaller section, just off the kitchen, is a good size for barbecuing, while the larger section can hold a table with chairs.

◀ A CUSHY GATHERING PLACE

Large leaves form a playful backdrop for the semicircular stone bench on this patio. A few added touches— chairs, lamps, and a coffee table— make this area the perfect conversation pit. The dark hues of the cushions contrast nicely with the bricks and stones.

◀ POOLSIDE PATIO AND PATH

The roughly rectangular patio stones are arranged in rows that follow the contours of a garden pool. Mortar between stones adds a prominent visual element. The stones that abut the pool are also mortared in place, but the mortar is recessed for a more natural look.

▼ SEVERAL SEATING AREAS This patio
is artfully shaped to accomodate three distinct sitting areas for groups of various sizes. A large area in the middle allows easy transitions from one group to another. Guests can choose to form intimate groups or join the general revelry.

RETREAT WITH A VIEW *A medium-sized space set amid trees and equipped with modest patio furniture can provide privacy, yet is ample enough to welcome guests. The patio stones have been cut to fit, making a crazy-quilt pattern. Low, mortared-stone walls delineate planting areas.*

▲ *A WIDE, WANDERING PATH* *A capacious path like this does double duty as a pleasant place to rest or to socialize. The short garden walls are at the right height for sitting. Large flagstones form ragged edges but are carefully cut to fit against each other and occasional boulders.*

▼ *ELEGANT GATEWAY* *Guests arriving for a dinner party are greeted with a lush view: A gate framed by potted flowers and well-placed beds opens to a pathway that is intimate but not crowded. The dining area is just the right size for a small gathering. The patio and low walls are made of mortared bricks of several hues.*

floors and paths

A masonry floor surface provides a smooth and natural transition between house and yard. Paths and patios act as extensions of your home, and also harmonize with your plantings. A horizontal surface at your feet does not usually draw close scrutiny, so it's fine to use rough materials with loose joints— for example, flagstone with soil-filled or loose gravel joints. If you want a more stately look, install bricks, concrete pavers, or tiles.

▲ **GEOMETRIC PATH AMID LOOSE STONES**
Large, round pebbles are beautiful but make a poor walking surface. The inset brick path is more practical (you can roll bikes or the garbage bin over it), and its geometric shape contrasts nicely with the surrounding stones and foliage. The bricks are set in a jack-on-jack pattern, and blue-stained accent bricks pick up the color of the pebbles. Bricks like these can be set in sand and held in place with invisible edging, or they can be mortared onto a concrete slab.

◀ **FLAGSTONES AMID PEBBLES** For a light-traffic path, a more casual arrangement—and simple installation—is possible. Here, small boulders form an edging; they are set firmly in soil, and the area between them is dug to a depth of about 4 inches. The soil is tamped, then a layer of attractive gravel is poured and tamped. Flagstones are placed at natural step intervals, and the resulting spaces are filled with a single layer of pebbles.

▲ **FLAGSTONE PATIOS** *Medium-sized stones congregate in tight groups to form a patio, then scatter to serve as steppingstones and then recongregate to form another patio. Two layers of heavy-duty landscaping fabric were placed under the patios to prevent the growth of weeds. The steppingstones are set at a height that makes it possible to mow over them while cutting the lawn.*

◄ **PATTERN OF PAVERS** *Concrete pavers with a natural stone look form an inviting grid of square sections. No pavers were cut for this installation. Each section is carefully sized to hold a single row of perimeter pavers; the pavers in the middle are laid in a basketweave pattern. One middle section is left empty to accommodate plantings.*

11

◀ GEOMETRY PLUS WHIMSY
This carefully designed patio makes the most of a small space. It's actually a concrete slab made with white Portland cement for a lighter color. A grid of evenly spaced control joints gives the impression of stone tiles. The flower patterns are made using stencils and concrete stain. The surface is well coated with acrylic sealer to keep it looking fresh for decades.

◀ **RAMBLING 'ROUND A FOUNTAIN**
Desert plants surround a raised garden pool creating the feel of a small oasis. On the ground, large stone tiles are arranged in a carefully planned pattern that leaves open spaces for plantings. If the perimeter plants will have large roots in this setting, the tiles should be set on a concrete slab to keep them from buckling.

◀ **PLANNED CHAOS** *Slate tiles of several hues, some of them cracked, give the impression of an ancient plaza. Smaller crevice plants grow in the joints. The corners of some tiles are broken to make room for larger plants.*

SPRAWLING SPACES *On a large surface, it is often most effective to use a simple pattern. An intricate design will tend to lose its focus with repetition. This patio is ringed with bricks laid on edge and mortared onto a concrete footing. The main patio bricks are laid in sand.*

◀ **RIVER OF STONE** Decorative gravel in an undulating pattern with occasional boulders and overhanging plants is reminiscent of a flowing river.

▼ **A BACKDROP FOR COLOR** Natural brick in several different hues is a serene backdrop for the bold splashes of color provided by flowering shrubs. These bricks are mortared onto a concrete slab, and the joints are filled with mortar.

vertical elements

Even if it's only a few feet tall, a structure that projects upward will be more noticeable than a patio or path. A short section of wall, a raised bed, or several planters can go a long way toward defining the look of your yard. A retaining wall usually leans back into the soil it retains, while a garden wall rises straight up. Most any masonry material—concrete blocks, bricks, natural stone, and even broken chunks of used concrete—can be either mortared together or stacked dry. When designing a vertical element, include plants in the plan; masonry walls almost always look better when partially covered with foliage.

▲ A BACKDROP FOR FLOWERS

*When plants are as showy as these
succulents, there's no harm in letting
them cover much of the stone wall.
In a cold climate, perennial crevice
plants may start small in the spring
and grow lush during the summer,
so choose late-blooming plants to show
off the wall at first and the flowers later.*

◄ RISING POOL WALLS
*Mortared
walls made of ashlar (cut stone) both
surround and project into a decorative
pond. The walls rise in height as they
march up the hillside. The lower walls
are capped with limestone, creating a
pleasantly situated bench.*

NATURAL ROCK GARDEN *Mimicking an
Alpine hillside, long boulders are positioned
in nearly parallel rows perpendicular to
the rise of the hill. Large plants were carefully
chosen for height, so that they and the
boulders are displayed to full advantage.*

▲ **RUSTIC ARCH** Building an arch is not as difficult as it looks, but it does take time. First, build firm walls on either side. (The entire structure is mortared, though the mortar is recessed so as to be nearly invisible.) Then construct a wooden brace in the shape of the bottom of the arch, and lay the stones in mortar on top of the brace. The stones will remain firmly in place when the brace is removed.

▶ **MIX-AND-MATCH STONE WALL** To build a wall like this, large boulders are first set using heavy machinery; then, flagstones are cut and dry-laid to fill in the spaces between. Boulders and flagstones cantilever out to provide ledges for plants or for sitting. Most of the large patio stones need to be cut on at least one side to achieve even joint lines.

◄ MORTARED STONE STEPS
Roundish stones assembled and joined with mortar make for steps that are slightly irregular. With careful construction, steps like these can be fairly consistent in height and depth, but they will not be as easy to walk on as most stairs.

▼ THE FEEL OF RUINS Structures that look like ancient ruins create a relaxed ambience. To build an adobe ruin like this, assemble the wall, then partially plaster it with adobe mix, and set stones in random locations. For a pitted appearance, blast the wall with water before it dries completely.

▶ **PICTURESQUE OPENING** *This stone wall appears to have been thrown together quickly, but it takes patience and plenty of time to lay irregular stones like these. A window requires an extra-long stone at the top of the opening.*

▼ **FAUX STONEWORK** *At first glance, these walls look like mortared natural stones. They are actually decorative concrete blocks, each made to look like seven or eight stones. Simply stack the blocks for easy installation.*

▲ **UNDULATING WALL** *Most walls are built level for a solid and steady appearance. For a more relaxed look, consider allowing the wall to follow the contours of the ground.*

▶ **PLANTER NOOK** *A small arch in a wall with a ledge at the bottom is just the spot for a potted plant.*

nice touches

It's easy to get so involved in the sweaty work of laying masonry that you lose track of your ultimate goal—to create an outdoor setting that is livable and pleasant. So, every once in a while, stand back, grab a drink, and ponder how you can make your yard unique. A few small decorative elements can have a visual impact that is out of proportion to their size. It may take only a trip to a resale shop and an hour or two of easy labor to add that touch of whimsy and make your space memorable.

▶ ***FOUND CONTAINERS*** *Old copper containers left uncoated acquire luscious, verdigris-green stains. Even rust spots on galvanized watering cans are appealing, though the rust will eventually cause leaks.*

▼ ***A SHORT STONE WALL*** *A babbling brook is enhanced by a short stone wall that barely looks man-made. Rock edging and a few well-placed boulders complete this rustic rural scene.*

▲ **SMALL BRIDGE** *This footbridge is cast concrete. Units like this are sometimes available at stone yards and at masonry supply centers. The trail is made of stones set on edge in a sand bed. The joints are filled with gravel, and invisible plastic edging holds it all together.*

◀ **ECLECTIC PLANTERS** *Clay sewer pipes make convenient planters for small plants. Bricks painted in two colors and upside-down Champagne bottles add to the whimsy.*

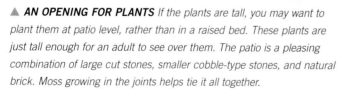 **AN OPENING FOR PLANTS** *If the plants are tall, you may want to plant them at patio level, rather than in a raised bed. These plants are just tall enough for an adult to see over them. The patio is a pleasing combination of large cut stones, smaller cobble-type stones, and natural brick. Moss growing in the joints helps tie it all together.*

▶ **FRAGRANT SEATING AREA** *Though they also form a stairway, these curved steps stand out as a wonderful place to sit and ponder. Aromatic herbs such as thyme and marjoram are incorporated in the design, making the air smell delicious.*

▼ **TOUCH OF ARTISTRY** *A handmade, stained-glass lamp is set into a masonry wall. Objects like this can be pricey, but it takes only one or two to add elegance.*

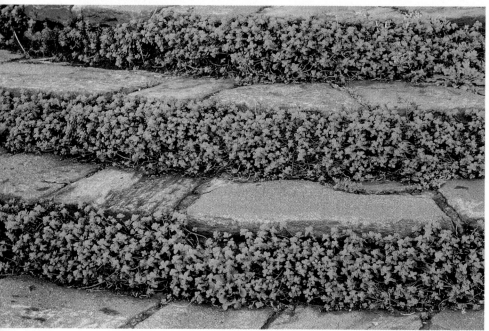

▲ **FOUNTAIN WITH POOL** *This opulent yet charming setting is made of components that are readily available. Decorative fountainheads can be found at pottery stores and garden centers. The plumbing can be installed by a landscaping or irrigation contractor.*

◄ **GENEROUS CREVICE PLANTINGS** *Some plants can grow large and lush with only a thin crack for access to soil. Choose plants that can rebound from being stepped on.*

CASCADING WATERFALL WITH POOLS *A water feature like this looks random but must be planned carefully so that the water flows where you want it to. An EPDM liner under the rocks keeps the water from soaking into the ground, and a pump recirculates the water for continuous flow. See Sunset's* Garden Pools, Fountains & Waterfalls *for more information.*

natural stone

Limestone, marble, sandstone, granite, slate, bluestone—the varieties, colors, and textures are extensive. Yet somehow any type of natural stone looks great when set next to green foliage, flowers, natural wood, or other masonry materials. Whether rough-textured and irregular, or smooth and neatly cut, stone never goes out of style.

Placing and installing natural stone is a matter of art as much as craft. Whether you are building a vertical or a horizontal surface, stand back once in a while and gaze at the assemblage. Often, a subtle shift here and there can make the difference between a sloppy arrangement and a stunning creation.

Natural stone also can be cut precisely into tiles (see page 30).

FLAGSTONE

Flagstone is not a species of stone, but rather it is a general term referring to large, flat stones that are 1 to 4 inches thick. Flagstone commonly is limestone, sandstone, or slate. Usually flagstone is made by splitting rather than cutting, and this gives it a characteristically rough surface that may be bumpy,

pitted, or composed of different mesalike planes. The surface offers excellent traction in wet conditions but makes it somewhat difficult to scoot a chair away from a table.

Most limestone is difficult to cut but strong; sandstone and slate are easy to cut and, predictably, are not as strong. A large slab of sandstone must be installed carefully, or it will crack when walked on. Pallets may or may not state the species of stone; experiment with a small sample piece to find out how hard it is.

Light tan is the most common color, but you can find flagstones in shades of gray and reddish brown, as well. At a masonry supply yard you will find large flagstones in one- to two-ton

pallets. A single pallet may contain stones of different colors and textures, even though they are of the same species. A ton of stones $1\frac{1}{4}$ inch thick will cover twice as much area as stones that average $2\frac{1}{2}$ inches thick.

A classic flagstone patio can be installed simply by excavating away sod and then setting the stones in tamped soil (see pages 50–51). Or, flagstones can be set in a bed of sand or even in mortar for greater stability.

Flagstones can be quickly stacked to form a short wall or a garden bed. Choose stones that are 3 inches thick or thicker and no wider than 16 inches.

COBBLESTONES

Cobblestones are roughly cut into squares or rectangles with rounded edges, generally from 6 to 12 inches square. Granite cobblestones are expensive but stunning and are often used for borders, accents, or small walks.

Cobblestones can be used for borders, accents, and walks.

Large, flat flagstones are perfect for paving patios or walkways. Also, they can be stacked to create low walls.

STONE FOR WALLS

A supplier may list a large variety of wall stone categories, but basically three types of stone are available for building walls. "Rubble," sometimes called "fieldstone," "boulders," or "river rock," is uncut stone and usually has rounded edges. It is inexpensive but difficult to stack. Use rubble for accents or a very low wall; don't try to build a rubble wall unless you have experienced and strong-backed help. "Semidressed stone" has been roughly shaped, at least on two sides. It can be stacked to form a stable wall, though you will need to experiment and to adjust it quite a bit as you work.

"Ashlar" is stone that has been fully trimmed, so it is nearly as easy to lay as brick. It may come in one or in several thicknesses. In a "coursed" ashlar design each course is composed of stones that are the same thickness. "Random" and "combination" ashlar walls combine stones of various thicknesses in patterns that resemble a patchwork quilt.

LOOSE STONE AND GRAVEL

Use loose materials for paths or patios in light-traffic areas. You'll find a wide range of colors, textures, shapes, and sizes at a stone supplier. Like larger stones, these complement any foliage and any natural wood.

Three types of stone used for building walls are, from top: rubble, semidressed, and ashlar.

Pebbles and beach stones are round and smooth, so they provide excellent drainage but do not compact well. Small stones with sharp edges, such as crushed granite, pea gravel, and Navajo rock, can be compacted with a drum roller or with a vibrating plate compactor to form a much more stable surface. Other types, such as red lava and white dolomite rock, fall in between.

stone tile

Natural stone cut into square or rectangular tiles creates a more formal-looking surface. Some types are cut as precisely as ceramic tiles; others are hand cut and vary in thickness and in width. Many stone tiles must be laid in a bed of mortar atop a solid concrete slab or they will crack; thicker and stronger types can be set in sand like bricks or pavers.

Check with the supplier about a stone tile's suitability for outdoor use in your area. Some may not be strong enough to withstand freeze-thaw cycles, and others may be slippery when wet or frosty. Some may be porous and prone to staining, rendering them unsuitable for a patio eating area unless they are coated with sealer. A stone or tile dealer should tell you the exact setting requirements for your type of tile.

Bluestone is quarried in New York and Pennsylvania but is increasingly available throughout the country. It has a rich blue-gray color unmatched by any other product. Some of these tiles are imbued with tinges of green, rust, yellow, and purple. Sometimes a single tile exhibits several hues. You can obtain bluestone tiles of various sizes for use as pavers (see pages 92–93). "Tread stock" is thick and strong

enough to be used as steps with minimal support. A thick slab also can be used as a countertop.

Slate tiles from all over the world, including India, Africa, and Mexico, come in a stunning array of colors. The texture is usually bumpy yet smooth; a single tile may be matte in some spots and shiny in others. Some types of slate are very hard and strong, while others are easily cracked; check with your dealer to make sure the slate you choose suits your needs. "Vermont slate" comes as a kit with a group of various-sized tiles that fit together in a defined pattern like a puzzle.

ceramic tile

If you're looking for splashes of color, or a patio surface as smooth as that of an indoor room, ceramic tile is your best choice. Visit several tile stores and contemplate the vast array of colors and shapes.

Be sure that the tiles and the installation materials will survive your climate. In most cases, ceramic tile must be set in a bed of mortar (usually, thinset mortar) atop a solid concrete slab. Latex-reinforced sanded grout is durable enough for most outdoor applications, especially if you apply a sealer every year or so.

Mexican Saltillos and terra-cotta tiles have a soft reddish glow that lends warmth to a patio. However, most types are suitable for warm climates only; with one hard freeze, they could crack.

Many glazed ceramic floor tiles survive even in harsh climates if they are properly laid. However, a high-gloss glaze is slippery when wet. Some types have a slightly bumpy surface for skid resistance.

Quarry tiles are unglazed and very hard, so their surface is skid resistant and durable. Their colors generally are limited to earth tones and pastels.

Modern methods produce porcelain tiles that are amazingly tough and easy to maintain. And porcelain can be made to resemble almost any type of ceramic or stone tile. While some people regard porcelain tile as an imperfect replica that lacks the true texture and natural beauty of stone or ceramic, others swear by the ease with which porcelain can be cleaned and its excellent stain resistance.

Mosaics are composed of many small tiles joined together, usually with a mesh backing. They are as easy to install as regular tiles. The tiles may be ceramic, stone, or porcelain.

Occasionally mixing in decorative tiles really can enliven a patio or path. Figure out how the decorative tiles will fit in with the design. If the plain field tiles need to be cut to accommodate the decorative tiles, consider having the tile supplier do the cutting for you.

brick

Essentially brick is still made the same way it has been since ancient time—firing a clay mixture in a kiln. The higher the firing temperature, the stronger the brick. The result of the process is a building block of rustic charm at home in any landscape. Brick is not as strong and weather resistant as are concrete pavers (see pages 34–35). But if you choose the right type, a brick patio or wall can last for centuries with little maintenance.

Especially in an area with freezing winters, many bricks that survive on walls will not survive as patio pavers, where they are subject to much more pressure. Some bricks designed to withstand freezing weather when used in walls are not suitable for use as pavers. Pavers are in contact with a lot more moisture than wall bricks. When the moisture freezes and expands, it can cause the bricks to crumble. For a patio, use bricks rated SX if your ground freezes; use bricks rated MX only in a warm climate. Consult with your dealer to make sure that the brick you buy will last. A coat or two of sealer will repel moisture and make bricks last longer, but it will not transform wall bricks into patio bricks.

A brickyard will offer a wide array of wall bricks. "Cored" bricks have three or more holes to reduce weight and to give the mortar greater grabbing power.

Wire-cut bricks have rough vertical lines; rough-facing bricks have the appearance of cracked earth. A fingerprint brick has several indentations that look like thumbprints. Bricks may be a single color, speckled, or composed of several slightly different hues. Used common bricks are often partially covered with white efflorescence.

Paving bricks, suitable for cold weather, are sometimes dark in color with a slightly glossy surface. A "frogged" brick has an old-fashioned indentation bearing the name of the manufacturer; you may want to scatter some of these throughout a patio. Faux "used" bricks are often concrete pavers made to look like old common brick.

ADOBE BLOCK

Traditional adobe block was made simply by mixing clay with straw, cutting it into slabs, and allowing it to dry in the sun. The resulting material needed to be covered with adobe plaster and could be used only in warm, dry climates. Today, asphalt emulsion or Portland cement is added to the mix to improve stability. These blocks can hold up even in cold climates, though they are not widely available outside the Southwest.

Adobe blocks are massive—4 × 8 × 16 and 4 × 8 × 8 are two common sizes. These large, earth-toned slabs look great in open garden spaces. Some types are irregular in shape, while others are manufactured with the same precision as bricks or concrete pavers. Adobe blocks can be laid in sand to form a patio, or they can be stacked to form a wall.

concrete pavers

In general, the term "paver" refers to any modular paving unit, such as a brick or an adobe block. A "concrete paver" is a type of paver made of dense, pressure-formed concrete. The result is an extremely durable paving material that can survive any climate. Because concrete pavers are precisely manufactured, they fit together tightly to form a surface that is relatively smooth.

Concrete pavers are usually less expensive than brick or stone, which makes them the obvious choice for many people. The faux appearance of some types—especially those with a pink hue—are unattractive to many people. However, newer styles come closer to the look of weathered natural stone.

"Interlocking" pavers have special shapes designed to fit together like a jigsaw puzzle. However, it is debatable whether simple rectangular pavers are any less stable. Choose interlocking types if you like the pattern.

Large pavers may be square, round, or hexagonal. They make attractive steppingstones. Some have an exposed-aggregate surface; others have a slightly raised pattern.

Some concrete pavers have a pinkish hue. Others more closely resemble natural stone or brick. You can buy a pallet that contains pavers of several different hues; the overall surface resembles natural cobblestone.

Some pavers come in ensembles of different sizes and shapes, as well as different hues, that form a rich pattern that looks like it would be complicated to install. However, laying such a grouping is not difficult. You don't have to plan the placement of all the pieces. Just maintain a fairly even distribution of the various sizes, and it's easy to make it come out right.

Circular and fan-shaped ensembles are also available. A circular ensemble may contain pavers in five or six different sizes and shapes. Follow the manufacturer's directions to create a circular or a semi-circular grouping. A fan pattern, also called an overlapping arc pattern, is reminiscent of European walkways; it also employs five or six different sizes of paver.

If you install pavers in a circular or fan-shaped pattern in a rectangular area, you will need to custom-cut quite a few pavers to fit along the edges. Use a wet masonry saw. Although the cuts will take time and patience, they won't be difficult to make.

CONCRETE BLOCK

Often incorrectly called "cinder block," concrete block offers a quick way to build a wall. Standard "stretcher" blocks typically have two large holes, or cells, that can be left open or filled with mortar for extra strength. Another type of concrete block interlocks so that the blocks can be set on top of each other to form a firm wall. The surface of either type of block can then be coated with a stuccolike surface bonding agent (see pages 148–53). In addition to stretchers, half blocks and cap blocks are usually needed.

Decorative concrete blocks offer an airy appearance and semi-privacy. Because they are only 3 inches thick and must be laid in a single wythe—the wall can be only one block thick—they should be reinforced with pillars at least every 8 feet (see pages 156–57).

STACKABLE RETAINING BLOCKS

Concrete stackable retaining blocks interlock to form a wall solid enough to keep a landscape or a garden bed firmly in place. Once you have excavated the area, stacking the blocks will likely take only a few hours.

envisioning your design

Begin the design process by gathering ideas; take the time to dream a bit. In addition to the designs shown in this book, look at yards in your neighborhood and note materials, structures, and layouts that appeal to you. Also, you may want to look at Sunset's Ideas for Great Patios and Decks and Complete Patio Book.

VISUALIZING TECHNIQUES

Have a family meeting and assess how you will use your yard. Those who entertain often with sit-down meals probably want room for a large table with chairs. Others may prefer a smaller space, perhaps with several other scattered sites for small groups to gather; large steps are ideal for this. If a play area for kids is important, locate it within view of adults. If solitude is important, plan a secluded spot for relaxing and reading the paper.

Even the most complete set of drawings may not give a clear idea of how the finished project will look and feel. So, use a hose or rope to mark the outline of a future patio on the lawn. Drive stakes and stretch string lines to indicate both the perimeter and the height of a proposed wall. Then set out the patio furniture— table and chairs, barbecue unit, perhaps with a table, as well as lounging furniture—to see how the layout feels. Have several family members participate and aim for an arrangement that provides ample space, yet creates a cozy gathering spot or two.

SOLVING PROBLEMS

Most people consider their yards to be less than perfect. Often what seems like a drawback offers exciting design possibilities. For instance, a heavily sloped lawn is uninviting, but offers the possibility of two or more patios on different levels or, perhaps, a wide stairway or a series of terraced garden beds. A small, flat yard with too-close neighbors can be transformed into a cozy retreat by installing masonry walls or large shrubs.

DEFINING AREAS AND PATHS

Think of your outdoor living space in terms of defined areas that are joined by paths. Though each situation is unique, here are some general rules of thumb:

- A dining area includes the table, plus from 36 to 48 inches for chair space on all sides.

ROUND OR SQUARE TABLE WITH CHAIRS

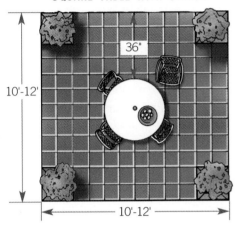

RECTANGULAR TABLE WITH CHAIRS

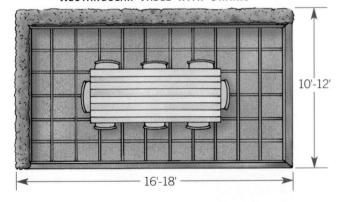

A typical round or square table requires an area 10 to 12 feet square. A rectangular table for eight diners calls for an area 10 to 12 feet by 16 to 18 feet.

- A lounge chair or hammock with a small end table for drinks will fit comfortably into an area about 4 feet by 8 feet.
- For a barbecue area, allow space for at least one small preparation table. A space 6 feet by 8 feet will fit a cook and a couple of advisers.

LOUNGE CHAIR WITH SMALL TABLE

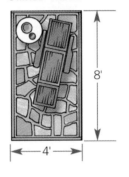

BARBECUE AREA

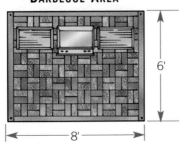

- Don't forget to make room for paths; they must be separate from the other defined areas. A 3-foot-wide path is sufficient for light traffic.

PLAN FOR LIGHTING

Well-placed lighting makes an outdoor living space usable at all hours and accents attractive features of your landscape. Plan lighting that is versatile. Lights that illuminate paths or that discourage intruders should be controlled by photo cells that turn on at night or by motion sensors. Lighting that illuminates a dining or lounging area should probably be controlled by a standard switch.

If you need bright illumination, or if you need to install an outdoor electrical outlet, have an electrician run standard cable, perhaps through a conduit, before you install your masonry projects. Take precautions to ensure that you will not damage the lines while you excavate or build.

Low-voltage lighting, available in convenient kits, can be installed easily by a homeowner either before or after the structures are built. Plug the timer into an outlet and run the thin lines in shallow trenches or staple them to the underside of structures. The lights themselves can usually be simply poked into the ground or screwed to a wood or masonry structure.

drawing plans

Time that you spend drawing plans will more than likely pay for itself in work saved later. A set of detailed and accurate plans will help you execute your design with fewer mistakes. And the actual process of drawing plans will help you spot and solve problems ahead of time.

WORKING WITH INSPECTORS

Your local building department has very specific requirements for all sorts of masonry structures. These requirements are based on decades of experience building in your locale. So, it is well worth your while to follow them, even if they slow construction and increase your material costs.

If a project does require inspection, you probably will need to present drawings and a materials list. Present scale drawings that are complete and make them as professional looking as possible. Once the inspector has approved the drawings, there will probably be two inspections, one for the excavation and perhaps for the installation of the base, and

another for the finished job. Be very clear on what should and should not be installed for each inspection. If you cover up anything that the inspector wants to see, you may be forced to tear up some of your work.

The inspector knows more than you do, so treat him or her with respect; it almost never pays to argue. Inspectors often have little patience with homeowners—they prefer working with pros. However, if you show that you are eager to follow instructions, the relationship will probably be friendly and helpful.

MAKING DRAWINGS

The simple drafting tools shown in the photo on page 36 greatly

ease the task of drawing plans. A clear drafting ruler enables you to draw perfectly parallel lines that are consistently spaced. For a simple radius curve, use a compass; use a bendable curved line tool for more complex curves.

If you have a survey drawing for your lot, you may want to enlarge the portion of it that you will be working on. At a copy center, experiment until you achieve a drawing that is exactly to scale—so, for example, one inch equals 10 or 20 feet. Make several copies to draw on.

If you have no survey, measure the area and make an accurate drawing. Graph paper sometimes helps keep things to scale. Sketch in trees and any permanent shrubs, as well as existing structures (see below).

When making a plan drawing (overhead view), be as specific as possible. Measure precisely and perhaps even draw patio bricks to scale. (If you will use

MAPPING MAJOR FEATURES

Plotting your design will be easier if you start with a basic yard drawing that includes features such as trees, boulders, and existing structures that you want to keep. Start with a drawing that is exactly to scale (see above).

Use triangulation to place features on the drawing: Measure from two widely spaced fixed points (such as corners of the house) to the feature. Use a calculator to convert the measurement to the scale of the drawing. (A construction calculator works in feet and inches rather than decimals and so saves hassle.) For example, if the scale is 1 inch to 10 feet, divide the distance in feet by 10 to get the number of inches on the drawing. For each measurement, set a compass to the correct distance and draw an arc. The intersection of the arcs marks the spot.

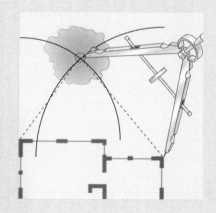

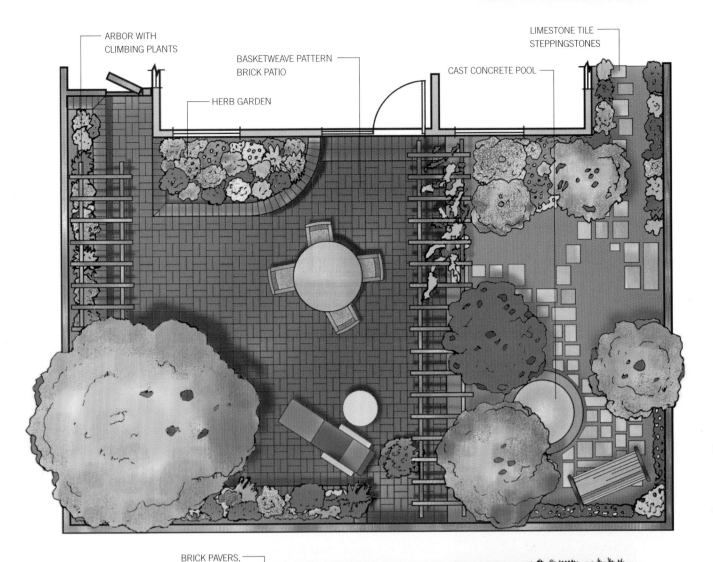

ARBOR WITH
CLIMBING PLANTS

BASKETWEAVE PATTERN
BRICK PATIO

HERB GARDEN

CAST CONCRETE POOL

LIMESTONE TILE
STEPPINGSTONES

BRICK PAVERS,
4" X 8" X 2½"

3" COMPACTIBLE
GRAVEL

1½" SAND

4 X 4 EDGING ANCHORED
WITH ⅜" REBAR EVERY 4'

interlocking pavers with odd shapes, you may choose to draw simple rectangles of the same size instead and make a note of the actual shape of the pavers.) If a patio or wall slopes, indicate the direction and the rate of slope.

It may help to draw patio furniture and large flower pots to scale on a separate sheet of graph paper and then cut them out. You then can set the furniture on the patio to get a realistic idea of spacing.

Also prepare detailed elevation (side view) drawings. These depict underlying structures, as well as surface materials, and show how things are put together. An inspector needs to know the depth of the excavation, the thickness of the gravel and sand beds, and the length of any reinforcing materials. Be sure to include any drainage solutions.

THE MATERIALS LIST

As you draw, make an exhaustive materials list. You need not figure how many patio pavers or wall bricks you need, but you should indicate how many square feet will be covered. Calculate the amount of gravel, sand, and mortar that will be needed and indicate the type of each material. If your list is accurate, it will save you extra trips to the brickyard.

rock garden basics

You might think that a rock garden can be made by strewing boulders and rocks in a random way that is "natural," but truly natural formations usually have a certain order to them. Stick to a single type of rock and choose stones close in their color. Think architecturally, to establish related lines and planes.

Boulders and large rocks usually look most natural if about one-third of each one is buried. Alternatively, sink a rock into the ground to just beyond its widest point.

You may be able to make a small rock garden using hand tools; see page 47 for lifting techniques. In most cases, however, you should hire a company to transport large boulders. Or, rent a small earth-moving machine (see page 63) that is capable of lifting and precisely placing the boulders.

BOULDERS WITH SCREE

A typical natural scree is a pile of broken stone lying at the base of a cliff. To mimic this look, first establish boulders near the top of the rock garden. Prepare the rest of the area for the plants of your choice. For plants that require excellent drainage, excavate to a depth of 18 inches and then add a mix of roughly equal parts sand, crushed rock, and soil to within an inch or two of grade. Cover the top inch with stones that match the color of the boulders.

BOULDERS IN A FIELD

To capture the look of boulders in an open field, choose rocks and boulders that are somewhat chiseled in appearance, rather than round. On a flat or gently sloped yard, lay stones and boulders in roughly parallel lines, all oriented in the same direction. The top of each stone should be on the same plane, and all should be slightly tilted at the same angle. The more harmonious the composition, the more restful the landscape will feel.

Stones are piled to mimic a scree at the bottom of a cliff.

SPLIT-BOULDER GARDEN

To simulate the ravages that time and weather work on stone, have a rock yard take a large boulder and split it lengthwise several times along its grain. Place the resulting slabs parallel and in order, but leave gaps of several inches between the slabs. Pack the gaps with a suitable soil mix and plant miniature gardens in each joint.

PLANTING A ROCK GARDEN

Choose perennials that require little maintenance and that thrive in very well drained soil. Good choices include succulents, dwarf conifers, mound-forming perennial flowers, slow-growing shrubs, miniature bulbs, and rhododendrons.

Buy plants in small pots and arrange the pots on the soil before you install the top layer of gravel. Plant each so that the top of the rootball is about ½ inch above the soil surface. Then spread the surrounding area with 1 inch of gravel. To add a plant later, clear away all the finish gravel before digging the hole, so that the gravel doesn't get mixed in with the soil. For more information on planting a rock garden, consult Sunset's *Landscaping with Stone*.

Hardy perennials look great planted between rocks.

crevice plants

Many nurseries have a special section for plants that can survive being walked on and can be planted in small cracks. Crevice plants add color and soften the appearance of a patio or wall.

Carefully choose plants that will survive. Desert plants like thyme and succulents need little moisture and can die if overwatered. The soil should be about half sand and should be well drained to a depth of at least a foot. If the patio is subject to puddling, the plants may have trouble surviving. Other plants require more moisture and do best when planted in a rich potting soil.

Be sure to remove all weeds completely before planting. Once established, many weeds (such as common grass) have roots that reach deep. So you may need to pull up a paver or stone in order to pull the whole plant out.

Some crevice plants are hardier than others. In general, larger plants survive well only in low-traffic areas; plants with small leaves are less crushable. Succulents look fragile, but some types are surprisingly hardy. Herbs like thyme and marjoram release a pleasant aroma when trod upon.

Buy plants rather than seeds; young shoots are very fragile.

The dense foliage of the Elfin variety of Thymus serpyllum is perfect between pavers.

On a patio, plant as you install the soil or sand to fill in the joints between pavers or flagstones. Break apart a plant into small portions and carefully dig deep enough so that the roots don't have to be balled up. Set the plants several inches apart, then fill around them with soil or sand. To plant on a wall, see page 159.

Above: *Purple verbena grows between steppingstones.* **Right:** *Ice plant, oregano, sedum "Vera Jameson," and aubrieta grow in a dry stone wall.*

lifting and carrying techniques

Even if you are in good shape, you probably will find that masonry work stresses joints and muscles—especially those in the lower back—in new ways. It is not only heavy lifting that can cause back strain. Repeatedly lifting and placing bricks and pavers, especially if you are on your knees (as you will be when laying a patio), may feel fine at the time but can cause pain the next morning. The same holds true for digging with a shovel or spade.

So, take it easy. Stand up and stretch every few minutes. Take plenty of breaks. Employ high schoolers for at least some of the grunt work. For a large excavation, hire a company or rent a small earth-moving machine (see page 63). Insist that heavy materials be delivered close to the site, even if it means paying a bit extra.

LIFT WITH YOUR LEGS Joints and muscles in the lower back are the most susceptible to long-term damage. When lifting a moderately heavy object, keep your back straight and bend your knees,

rather than bend your back. A lifting belt can help prevent strain.

USE A RAMP To raise a large stone into position without actually picking it up, make a simple 2 × 12 ramp, with 2 × 2 cross pieces screwed to it every 16 inches or so. The cross pieces will keep rocks from sliding back.

USE A HAND TRUCK To transport boulders, large stones, concrete blocks, or heavy bags, a hand truck is highly recommended. A model with air-filled tires is easier to push and less likely to damage

a lawn. If your truck has solid tires, lay a path of 2 × 12 or plywood strips on the lawn. Work with a helper to load the stone, then tilt it back until you feel no pressure on the handles.

patios and paths

A DURABLE, STABLE OUTDOOR FLOOR CAN BE MADE WITHOUT concrete or mortar, by laying brick or concrete pavers or flagstones on a firmly tamped bed of gravel and sand. The dry-laid projects shown in this chapter require no special skills or heavy lifting and can be completed in easy stages. ■ Plan delivery of materials so as to minimize strain to your back and damage to your yard. Ideally, the gravel and sand should be poured directly into the patio area. ■ Place the pavers within easy reach. Avoid placing them on the lawn, especially if it will take several weekends to complete the project. ■ Once you have determined the contours of your patio or path and have selected a paving material (see pages 28–39), consult with local builders or with your building department to plan a firm subsurface, so that your patio will not buckle after a year or two. Your building department may, or may not, want you to have a permit.

simple flagstone patio

Flagstones can be set in sand (see pages 80–83) or mortared onto a concrete slab (pages 126–27). But the simplest method, shown here, is to lay the stones directly on tamped soil. The flagstones themselves are the only materials you need to buy. You could install edging first, but then you would have to cut the flagstones to fit around the perimeter, and irregular edges are more in keeping with this informal approach.

A flagstone patio, no matter how it is laid, will be relatively rough and uneven, but smooth enough for most outdoor activities.

Choose flagstones that are fairly consistent in thickness; otherwise, it will be difficult to achieve an even surface. A stone yard may allow you to hand-pick flagstones for a small patio, but for a surface larger than 100 square feet, you probably will need to buy a pallet of stones. Flagstones are sold by the ton, so you can save plenty of money by buying thin stones—typically, about $1\frac{1}{4}$ inches thick.

Have the stones delivered as close to the site as possible; set them on sheets of plywood to protect the lawn. Sort the stones into three piles according to size; make a separate pile for narrow pieces. Choose stones from each pile as you lay the patio, so that stones of various sizes will be evenly distributed.

Though this is the simplest patio construction method, you must excavate correctly, so that the stones will remain stable for years. Remove all sod and any roots more than half an inch thick. Make sure the stones will

be slightly lower than the adjacent lawn, so that you can run a lawn mower over them.

1 Excavate, Tamp, and Rake

A small amount of rainwater will soak into the joints between stones, but to ensure against puddles on the patio during a heavy rain, slope the excavation away from the

house. Scrape, rather than dig, the bottom of the excavation, so that you will not loosen the undisturbed soil. Tamp the area with a hand tamper or power tamper, then gently rake to loosen a layer of soil about $\frac{1}{2}$ inch thick.

2 Cut Flagstones as Needed

See page 76 for cutting techniques. Sandstone will cut easily, while limestone will be tough to crack. If you have some very large stones, you may choose to keep them large and to space them regularly for a dramatic effect. Or, score each large stone with lines and break it apart. The resulting pieces can be laid with neat joints.

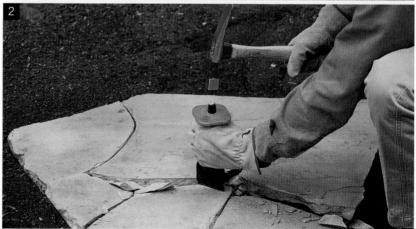

3 **Arrange Stones in a Dry Run**

Place the stones in the excavated area and experiment with different arrangements. Aim to achieve joints that are fairly consistent in width—between $\frac{1}{2}$ inch and 1 inch. This will take some time, so be patient. If a stone protrudes beyond the excavated area, you may choose to dig away the sod rather than to cut the stone.

4 **Set the Flagstones**

Once you have arranged about 10 square feet, set the stones before moving on to the next section. To set a stone, stand on it or tap it with a rubber mallet to produce an impression in the soil. Tilt the stone up and use a garden trowel to scrape and fill as needed. Lay the stone back down and test for stability. Probably it will take several attempts before the stone is free of wobbles and is level with its neighbors. If you have trouble stabilizing the stone, try adding sand as well as soil.

5 **Fill Joints with Soil**

Once all the stones are firmly set, slip soil into the joints using a pointed shovel or a garden trowel. Because this soil gets tightly compacted, it is often best to mix some sand with potting soil, to produce a soil that is firm but drains readily. Use soil that is slightly damp; wet soil will be hard to clean, and dry soil will compress a great deal when it is moistened. Allow the soil to dry. Then gently sweep the stones until they are clean.

6 **Spray and Refill**

Set a nozzle to produce a fine mist and spray the patio until the joints are soaked. This will compress the soil. Wait for the soil to dry, add more soil as needed, and spray again. If you choose, sprinkle seeds, brush with a moss mixture, or embed crevice plants (see pages 42–43).

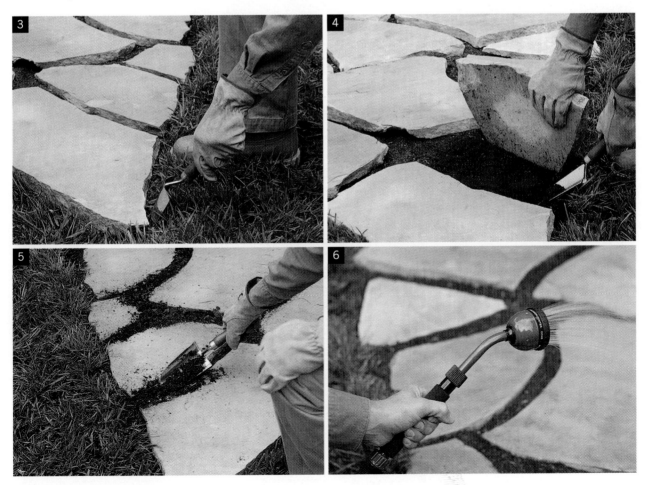

placing steppingstones

This is an easy way to create a decorative path for a light-traffic area. (For a more surefooted path, install a path made of edging-enclosed pavers or loose materials (see pages 89, 94–95).

happens, simply tilt it up and scrape or fill the soil beneath it as needed. If the problem persists, you may want to add sand.

ARRANGING THE STONES

There are two approaches to steppingstone placement. The method shown below allocates one stone per adult step. Another approach is to make a path 3 feet wide, with consistent joints between the stones, using the techniques shown on pages 50–51.

Stretch mason's line to lay out a straight path, or use two hoses to outline a curved path. A stepping path should be about 2 feet wide. Place the stones within the two lines or hoses alternating right to left. Have family members walk on the stones to determine the most comfortable arrangement.

On a manicured lawn, steppingstones will be fully exposed. In other settings, nearby plants will most likely partially cover the steppingstones. Read about the plants you are using to determine how invasive they will be and buy larger stones, so that you will still have a usable path after the plants have grown.

The steppingstones above are irregular flagstones, but you can also buy precast concrete steppers in uniform square, octagonal, or round shapes. These may be smooth and colored, or they may have exposed-aggregate surfaces.

After a year or two, a stepping-stone may become wobbly. If this

SETTING THE STONES

Steppingstones can simply be set in tamped soil, but adding a bit of sand makes the installation easier.

1 Slice the Stone's Outline

One method is to leave the stones on the lawn for a week; when you pick them up, the yellowed grass will show you where to cut. Stepping or tapping on a concrete paver will press the shape into the grass. Or, set the stone in place and use a shovel to slice a line through the sod around the stone.

2 Remove Sod and Dig the Hole

Dig up and remove the sod under the stone. Remove all organic material, including any roots. Dig deep enough so that after adding $\frac{1}{2}$ inch of sand the stone will be just below grade—low enough so that you can run a lawn mower over it. Tamp the soil firm, using a 2 × 4.

3 Add Sand and Bed the Stone

Add about $\frac{1}{2}$ inch of damp sand and spread it. If the stone is uneven in thickness, roughly mirror the stone's contours with the sand. Set the stone in place. If it is too high, dig the hole deeper. Tap the stone with a rubber mallet or step on it.

4 Reshape the Sand and Replace the Stone

Tilt the stone up to reveal voids and high spots. Scrape the high spots and fill the voids with sand; then replace the stone. Walk on the stone. If it wobbles even slightly, pick it up and add or scrape the sand where needed.

forming decorative steppingstones

Here is an enjoyable way to create one-of-a-kind features that are practical as well as charming. Homemade steppingstones can be a fun family project. You could do the serious work of making the form and casting the concrete and allow youngsters to make the patterns. If the kids lay out their patterns first, you can monitor the designs. The next two pages show some design options, but don't hesitate to use your imagination.

BUILDING THE FORMS

These steppingstones are pentagonal and are 14 to 16 inches wide, but you may choose to make yours a different size or shape. To speed up production, construct two or more forms. Build the forms from 1 × 2s. When constructing a pentagonal form, cut both ends of each of the five pieces at 72-degree angles. Screw together all but two of the pieces. Fasten

them with a hook and eye at two corners to make it easy to unmold the form. Place each form on a piece of plywood and spray oil onto all the surfaces that will touch concrete. (Spray cooking oil works fine.)

For each steppingstone, lay out the decorative elements on a piece of cardboard, so that you can quickly transfer them to the wet concrete. To ensure against cracking, purchase dry-mix bags of "high-early" concrete and cut pieces of metal stucco lath to fit within the forms; there should be a gap of about ¾ inch between the lath and the form at all points. You may choose to mix in concrete colorant; white dry-mix will make the colors more intense. See pages 116–17 for tips on coloring concrete.

FORMING AND FINISHING THE STEPPINGSTONES

Mix the concrete to a fairly stiff consistency, so that it nearly holds a ball shape when you squeeze it with your hands. Pour concrete into a form; overfill the form slightly. Smooth the top of the steppingstone with a magnesium or wood float. Use a concrete edger at the edges, or work these with a trowel. The concrete should be nearly as smooth as you want it to be before you set in the designs.

Once the designs have been set, cut through the gap between the boards and the concrete. Gently remove the boards. If the

concrete starts to sag, push the boards back into place and wait 5 or 10 minutes for the concrete to harden further.

After unmolding, brush the surface with a paintbrush or a mason's brush to achieve a uniform texture. The decorative elements may be covered with a thin film of cement, which you will wash off later.

SETTING DESIGNS

Add decorative elements soon after the bleed water has completely disappeared. If the concrete is too mushy, remove the decorative elements, retool the surface, and wait 10 minutes or so before trying again. Once the designs are in place, remove the forms and smooth the steppingstones' edges.

LEAF IMPRINT Select leaves with large, prominent veins. Carefully press each leaf fairly deep into the concrete, so that its outline breaks the surface. Either peel the leaves away immediately to see what the

impression looks like or leave them in place and allow them to decompose after a week or two.

STONES If pebbles or decorative stones are dry and porous, soak them in water briefly before placing them. To ensure that stones are solidly embedded, press them into the concrete slightly deeper than you want them; you can brush away some surface concrete once it begins to harden.

CARVING INITIALS For a classic naughty-kid look, have children scratch their initials into the concrete, using a small stick. For a more polished appearance, use the rounded edge of a tool or butter knife handle. It may take some practice before the kids get the hang of it.

PRESSED DESIGNS A wide variety of objects make interesting impressions. Experiment with tennis shoes, shells, action figures, and memorabilia. Choose objects with designs that make imprints at least $1/8$ inch thick. Some rubber stamps meet this criterion. To make a perfect handprint, wait 5 minutes after all bleed water is gone, make sure the hand is dry, and press firmly.

TILE SHARDS To safely break a tile, place it in a canvas bag, place the bag on a hard surface, and tap the bag with a hammer. Bright colors make the best designs. Handle the shards with care and sand or file down any sharp edges. Embed the shards deep in the concrete, so that only the surface is exposed; otherwise, the steppingstone could be unsafe for bare feet.

FINISHING AND USING THE STONES

Wait two days or more for the concrete to cure, then apply two coats of acrylic sealer. Set the steppers in soil or sand, as you would other steppingstones (see pages 52–53).

molded concrete

At a home center or a masonry supply source you can find plastic molds for forming concrete into shapes that resemble bricks or flagstones. These molds do simplify the process of forming concrete into attractive shapes, but don't expect them to automatically produce perfect shapes. Expect to spend a good deal of time smoothing the rough edges. You may choose to tint the concrete (see pages 116–17).

To ensure against cracking, excavate, spread compactible gravel, and power-tamp the gravel (see pages 60–63). There is no need for edging or a layer of sand. Ideally, the excavated area should be the right length to accommodate full-sized formed sections.

1 Pour into the Mold

Set the mold on the gravel and press it down so that the concrete cannot seep out the sides. Mix a fairly stiff batch of concrete; if it pours easily, it is a bit too wet. Shovel the concrete into the mold and take care to fill each cavity.

2 Trowel

Use a magnesium or a wood float to level the surface. Run the float across the form in at least two directions, fill in any voids, and level again. The float should scrape the plastic mold as you work.

3 Remove the Mold and Finish

Once all the bleed water has disappeared, carefully lift the mold straight up; you may have to gently shake it as you lift. Watch carefully; if one of the steppingstones starts to crack and fall apart as you lift it, press the mold back down into place and wait 10 minutes or so before trying again. Smooth rough edges, using a mason's brush or a paintbrush.

The resulting joints can be left as is, or you can fill them with sand or mortar.

laying out a patio

Once you have determined the general outline of your patio (pages 36–37), it's time to mark the perimeter precisely. Depending on the type of edging you will install, you may need to mark for two outlines—the actual outside of the patio (including any edging) and the area from which sod must be removed. This may be 2 inches or so past the patio perimeter, depending on the edging you choose.

USING BATTERBOARDS

A patio can be laid out quickly using lines attached to stakes, but it is well worth the small amount of time it takes to build and use batterboards instead. Batterboards are not easily bumped out of position, and they make it easy to adjust string lines and to remove and later replace them. Make a batterboard (like the one shown here) by attaching a 2-foot-long 1 × 4 to two 1 × 2 stakes. Make the stakes about 18 inches long. They should be longer if the ground is very soft or shorter if the ground is very hard.

Estimate the outline of the patio. Pound two batterboards into the ground about 2 feet beyond the estimated location of each corner, one on each side of the corner. If the patio will have a rounded edge, position the batterboards 2 feet beyond where the straight lines would intersect.

CHECKING FOR SQUARE

It's important for a rectangular patio to have square corners; otherwise, you will end up making lots of extra cuts, and the patio will look unprofessional.

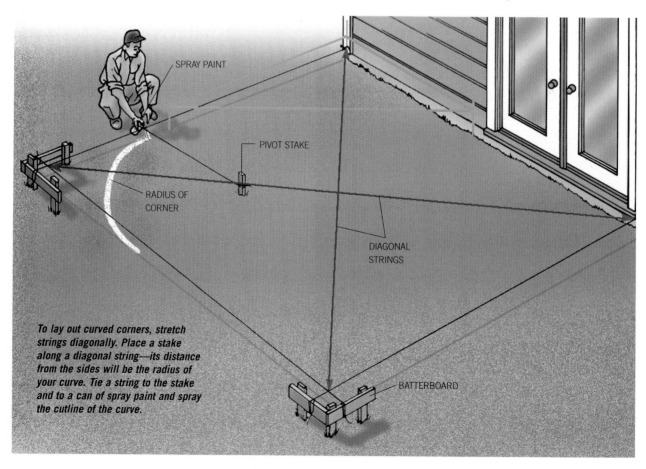

SPRAY PAINT

PIVOT STAKE

RADIUS OF CORNER

DIAGONAL STRINGS

BATTERBOARD

To lay out curved corners, stretch strings diagonally. Place a stake along a diagonal string—its distance from the sides will be the radius of your curve. Tie a string to the stake and to a can of spray paint and spray the cutline of the curve.

1 Stretch Mason's Line

Against the house, drive one nail or pound one stake to indicate the perimeter of the patio and another one to indicate the line where sod must be removed. Tightly stretch mason's line (not regular string, which is liable to stretch out) from the house to the batterboard on both sides of the patio. The strings should be close to the ground but should not touch the ground at any point. Temporarily wrap the lines around the batterboards, so that you can easily shift their positions. For the line that is parallel to the house, measure to position both ends the same distance from the house.

2 Measure for 6-8-10

To check a corner for square, mark a spot on the house precisely 6 feet from the corner. Use a piece of tape to mark the adjacent string precisely 8 feet from the corner. If the distance between the two marks is precisely 10 feet, then the corner is square. If not, move the string as needed. If the patio is large, use multiples of 6, 8, and 10 (such as 12, 16, and 20 or 18, 24,

and 30). Check the other corners using the same method.

Double-check by measuring the diagonals, which should be the same length. Once you are certain of the lines' positions, nail or screw them in place on the batterboards, and mark the batterboards for the positions of the outside of the patio and the area to be excavated.

3 Mark a Corner

If the lines attached to the batterboards are only a few inches from the ground, leave them in place and use them as guides for excavation. If the lines are high, they could be difficult to use as guides, so establish lines nearer the ground. First, mark the exact location of a corner: dangle a plumb bob (or a chalk line) so that its string nearly touches the intersection of the two layout lines and the weight is nearly resting on the ground. Drive a stake into the ground or dig out a bit of sod, to mark the exact corner. Then drive stakes and stretch lines near to the ground to mark the exact perimeter.

MARKING A CURVED SIDE

To create a curved side, lay a garden hose on the ground in the desired shape. Pour sand over the hose all along its length. When you pick up the hose, a clear outline will be revealed.

removing sod, excavating, and laying gravel

The following instructions show how to lay a substrate that is acceptable to most building departments and is sure to produce a strong surface in most soils: Excavate to undisturbed soil, lay and power-tamp 4 to 6 inches of compactible gravel, and screed an inch or so of sand on top.

However, depending on your soil conditions and climate, you may not need this deep layer of gravel and can simply tamp the soil firm and screed an inch or two of sand on top. Check with a pro or with your building department to find out how thick the gravel and sand should be in order to solidly support a patio in your area.

PLANNING THE EXCAVATION
Carefully think through your patio installation step by step. Often, the best sequence is: (1) remove sod and all organic material, (2) install edgings at the finished height of the patio, and (3) string a grid of guide lines across the edgings and excavate the interior of the patio to the correct depth.

However, if you will be installing a decorative edging that is uneven, first set up temporary 2 × 4 guides at the patio height and use them to measure for the depth of excavation. Do the same when excavating for a concrete slab (see page 108).

If the area will receive a lot of rain, or if it is larger than 500 square feet, you may need to provide drainage (see pages 64–65).

In most cases, it is best to install a patio slightly below grade, so that you can run a lawn mower over it. If the yard is uneven, you may need to fill in low spots with soil and sod that

were removed from the patio area. Some edgings require a trench that is deeper than the rest of the excavation; others are no deeper than the general excavation.

Decide where to place the excavated sod and soil. You may be able to use one or both somewhere in your yard. If not, advertise in a local paper; someone may be happy to haul it away.

TIP: LEAVE ONE SIDE OPEN

To minimize the need to cut patio pavers, hold off on the edging for one or two sides. Temporarily install 2 x 4s as a height guide. Once you have laid all or most of the pavers, you can install the final section of the edging snug against the last row (see page 87, step 5).

MORTAR-ON-GRAVEL SUBSTRATE

Another installation method calls for spreading an inch or so of wet mortar on the gravel bed and laying pavers in the mortar. This adds strength and is especially appropriate when installing large stones. However, a gravel-and-sand bed produces a durable surface and is easier to install.

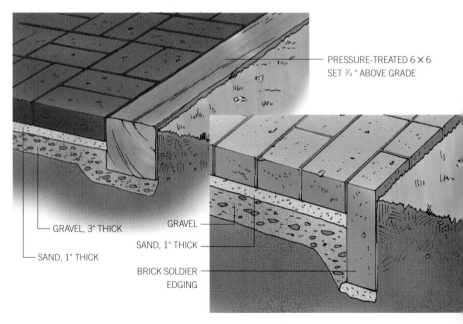

PRESSURE-TREATED 6 × 6 SET ¾" ABOVE GRADE

GRAVEL, 3" THICK

SAND, 1" THICK

GRAVEL

SAND, 1" THICK

BRICK SOLDIER EDGING

CUTTING SOD

For a small patio, dig up sod with a square shovel (above right). Cut a line around the perimeter, holding the shovel blade straight vertically. Slice a parallel line about 18 inches inside the patio; then undercut the sod between the two lines and pry the sod out.

For a larger area, rent a power sod cutter (above left) or buy a foot-operated sod cutter. These tools make the task much easier, though there will still be plenty of hard digging. Also, they make it easier to slice straight lines.

MEASURING FOR LEVEL AND SLOPE

Once the sod is cut, move the guide lines over to indicate the perimeter of the edging. At each corner, pound stakes firmly into the ground directly below the string lines. You will stretch mason's lines between the stakes to indicate both the perimeter and the height of the edging.

A patio should slope down and away from the house at ¼ inch per foot; where it is parallel to the house, the patio should be level. On the house, mark a level reference line to indicate the finished height of the patio—about 1 inch below the bottom of the door's threshold.

First, mark the corner stake for level. If the patio is 16 feet wide or less, check for level with a carpenter's level on a long, straight board (bottom left). To measure a longer distance, use a line level or a water level. Then measure down ¼ inch per foot and attach the string line at that point (bottom right). The line and the stake may get bumped, so check it from time to time.

EXCAVATE TO DEPTH

Install either the finished edging (pages 66–73) or temporary 2 × 4s staked at the finished height of the patio. You will use the edging as a guide for the depth of the excavation, so take care that the edging is firmly attached; check it once in a while to make sure that it has not been bumped out of position.

A patio substrate should rest on undisturbed soil, which is firmer than soil that has been dug up and replaced. So, make it your goal to excavate to the exact required depth and no farther.

To calculate the depth of excavation, add together the thickness of the gravel, the sand, and the finish material. A typical paver installation calls for 3 to 4 inches of compacted gravel and 1 inch of sand. For a concrete slab, it is common to have 3 inches of gravel plus 3 inches of concrete. However, consult with a local contractor or

your building department to be sure your installation will be firm enough.

Stretch a grid of mason's line across the edging, spacing the lines 4 to 5 feet apart in both directions. If the edging is wood, simply drive nails or screws and tie the lines to them. If the edging is brick, tie the lines to stakes driven a foot or two outside the patio, so that the lines rest on top of the bricks. Pull the lines very taut.

Your shovel blade may be the correct length to use as a depth guide. If not, mark the depth with a piece of tape on the handle. That way, you can quickly check for depth as you work. Dig first with a pointed shovel, then use a flat shovel to scrape the bottom.

All organic material must be removed from the site, including any roots over $\frac{1}{2}$ inch in diameter. If the organic material is left in place, the patio could buckle in time.

ADD AND TAMP GRAVEL

Order compactible gravel (also known as aggregate base course or hardcore), made to serve as a patio substrate. To figure how much you need in cubic yards, see page 105. If possible, have the supplier dump the gravel directly into the excavated area. Otherwise, you will need to use wheelbarrows.

Remove the guide lines. Rent a vibrating plate compactor an hour or two before the gravel will be delivered, so that you can power-tamp the soil first and then the gravel. Also, you may rent this machine to tamp the finished paver surface. (See page 86.)

Spread the gravel with a shovel, then rake it. Reinstall the guide lines and check for depth; note that tamping could lower the depth by about $\frac{1}{2}$ inch. Remove the lines, power-tamp several times for firmness, and recheck the depth.

EXCAVATING WITH A RENTED EARTH-MOVING MACHINE

Digging by hand is strenuous; if the ground is hard and the patio large, it may not be practical to do so. A small earth-moving machine, often referred to as a scooper or cat (short for the brand name Caterpillar), can be rented for about $200 per day. It will take an hour or two of practice to become reasonably proficient. Have the rental staff instruct you thoroughly in handling the machine. You may have to pay a fee to have the machine delivered and picked up.

Do not pre-install your finished edgings if you are using an earth-mover; you risk damaging them. Install temporary 2 x 4 edging, which you may have to remove and replace several times during excavation. Because you cannot operate the machine with guide lines in place, stop frequently to check for depth to ensure that you don't dig down too far.

Because these small machines are so maneuverable, they can be be practical for excavating areas as small as 100 square feet. You will be sitting low enough to see the machine's blade. Some models have treads or wheels that can turn in opposite directions, making possible extremely tight turns.

A small earth-mover is not heavy enough to cause deep ruts in a lawn with its wheels or treads, but it can do some damage. Lay out a plywood path wherever the machine will run on the yard.

Start by scooping—moving forward to dig up soil. Unload the soil at its final destination immediately. Avoid having to move the soil twice. Finish by scraping—moving backward while running the scooper's blade along the bottom of the excavation. The machine's wheels or treads can be used to tamp the soil firm.

Scoop carefully; you don't want to dig deeper than the thickness of the pavers and the substrate.

Off-load the excavated soil.

Scrape the bottom of the excavation using the back of the scooper.

drainage solutions

If your site had no discernable drainage problems before you begin the project, and the patio will be no wider than 16 feet, you may have no need for special drainage measures. If a minor problem arises after the patio is in place, it can be addressed by digging a trench and filling it with mulch.

However, be aware that unless a patio has wide soil-filled joints between the pavers, nearly all rainwater will flow to its edge—usually, the edge farthest from the house. Very little water will seep through the tight, sand-filled joints of a typical patio. So, if the site already develops puddles, expect accumulation at the edge of the patio's downward slope. The larger the patio, the more water will collect. Abdrainage system may be necessary.

PERIMETER TRENCHES

A gravel-filled trench will handle an average puddle problem. Either before or after constructing the patio, dig a 12-inch-deep trench and fill it with decorative gravel or pebbles. For greater drainage, lay a perforated drainpipe in the trench, sloped so it carries water away from the area during a severe rain. The drainpipe can simply meander through the lawn (water will trickle through the perforations). Alternatively, it can poke through to daylight at a hillside or end in a dry well (opposite page).

Running a drainpipe over long distances is best accomplished by a professional contractor with knowledge of local soil conditions and equipment to do the job quickly and neatly.

If you don't like the look of gravel, dig the trench 16 inches deep and fill it with pebbles or stones (not compactible gravel) that allow for easy drainage up to within 4 inches of the top. Place a layer of landscaping fabric over the gravel, fill with soil, and plant grass seed or lay sod.

PERIMETER TRENCH WITH EXPOSED GRAVEL

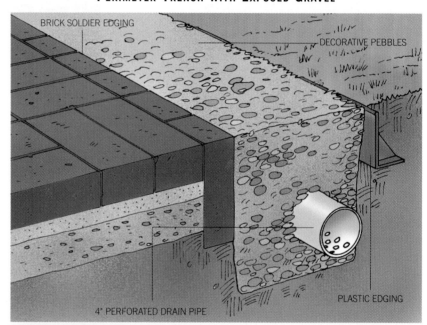

BRICK SOLDIER EDGING

DECORATIVE PEBBLES

PLASTIC EDGING

4" PERFORATED DRAIN PIPE

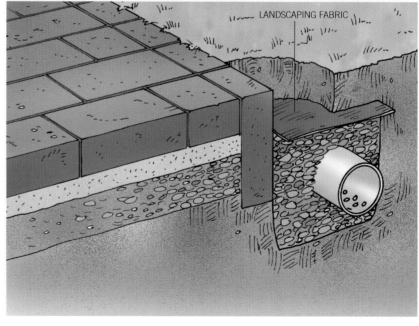

LANDSCAPING FABRIC

CATCH BASIN

To solve a severe drainage problem—if the patio is very large or if there is no good place to which the water can flow—consult with a contractor to see if you need a catch basin. If you do, the patio should be sloped toward a spot near the middle rather than the edge. At that middle spot, install a cylindrical or rectangular catch basin. An underground drainpipe will carry water away.

DRY WELL

A drainpipe may end at a dry well, which is simply a large hole filled with gravel. A dry well about 3 feet wide and 3 feet deep will hold a good deal of water, which will slowly percolate into the surrounding soil. Making a dry well requires no special skills. Dig the hole and run sloped drainpipe into it. Fill the hole with coarse gravel or pebbles. (Don't use compactible gravel.) Cover the hole with three layers of roofing felt (tar paper) topped with soil and sod.

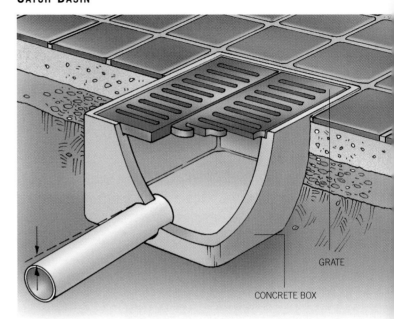

GRATE

CONCRETE BOX

DRY WELL

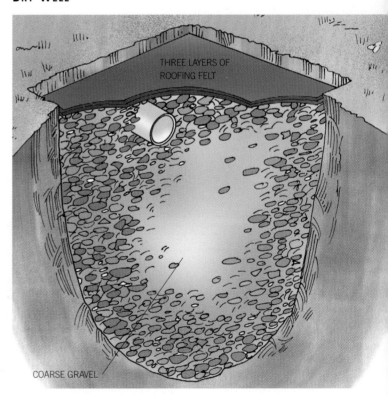

THREE LAYERS OF ROOFING FELT

COARSE GRAVEL

SOLVING DRAINAGE PROBLEMS IN AN EXISTING PATIO

If water often puddles on a concrete or paver patio, it is more than just a nuisance. It can damage the patio, especially if the water freezes. Creating a drainage solution will call for some sweaty work, but it might not be as difficult as you may think.

Determine the location(s) of the low spots, where the puddles are deepest. At each low point, cut an opening in the patio about 12 inches in diameter. If the patio is concrete, cut first with a saw or grinder (see pages 177 and 178), then chop it away with a chisel and a hammer. If the patio is masonry, remove as many pavers as needed.

Use a posthole digger to dig a hole at least 36 inches deep; you can enlarge the bottom of the hole. Fill the hole with coarse gravel. Install a drainage grate when you patch over the gravel.

wood edging

Thin wood edging—made with 2-by lumber or benderboard—adds a subtle touch; for a more dramatic effect, use timbers (see page 69). Pressure-treated lumber rated "ground contact" is durable and inexpensive. The dark heartwood of redwood is better looking but is expensive and not as resistant to rot. Light-colored redwood or cedar will likely rot within a couple of years.

TWO-BY EDGING

Select 2 × 4 or 2 × 6 boards that are straight and free of large knots. If possible, buy long boards so that you can avoid butt joints. If you cut a board, apply a generous coat or two of sealer to the cut end.

The edging must be supported with stakes every 2 feet or so. Cut the sod back 2 inches from the outside of the edging to make room for the stakes. Excavate deep enough to place 2 to 3 inches of rough gravel or pebbles under the boards.

1 Set the Boards in Place

Cut the boards to length and set them in place; rest the boards on gravel at either end. Check the guide strings and use a level to make sure the boards are at the right height and are either level or correctly sloped. You may need to shift gravel or to tap a board down. Sight along each board to make sure it is straight.

2 Drive Stakes

Cut stakes from pressure-treated 2 × 4s. The pointed tips should be about 4 inches long. The length of the stakes depends on soil conditions; it should take some effort to drive them to the desired depth. Use a 2 × 4 scrap, as shown, to prevent splitting the stakes. Drive stakes about 1½ inches below the top of edging boards. If the soil is very hard, or if the wood stakes tend to move the edging out of alignment, metal stakes may be the solution.

3 Drive Screws and Backfill

Check again that the edging is correctly aligned. From inside the excavation, drive two 2½-inch deck screws into each stake. Shovel gravel under the edging, to support it at all points. (This will prevent the wood from soaking in standing water.) Backfill with soil and lightly tamp with a 2 × 4; take care not to nudge the edging out of alignment. After the patio is laid, tamp the soil more firmly.

CURVED WOOD EDGING

For appearance sake, you may want curved edging to be the same thickness as any 2-by edging it abuts. For gentle curves, you may be able to use 1 × 4s. Redwood benderboard, about ⅜ inch thick, makes tight bends but is difficult to find in some areas. A lumberyard may rip-cut benderboard pieces out of pressure-treated 2 × 4s for a modest price. Plastic-composite decking boards are fairly bendable and may be close enough in color.

Because you cannot accurately measure the length of a curve, install pieces that are longer than you need and cut them to length after they are fully installed.

1 Bend the Boards in Position

Drive stakes, 1½ inches below the top of the edging, at the beginning and at the end of the curved run, on the outside of the benderboard (that is, the side outside the patio). Bend the board to the desired shape and drive temporary stakes on the inside to hold the edging in place.

2 Install Permanent Stakes

Use a carpenter's level to check that the edging is level or correctly sloped. Every 2 feet, drive a permanent stake on the outside so that its top is 1½ inches below the top of the edging. Drill pilot holes and drive deck screws to attach the benderboards to the permanent stakes. Remove the temporary stakes.

3 Cut the Ends

At the point where the curve ends and a straight line begins, use a small square to draw a cutoff line. Cut the curved edging, using a handsaw or a reciprocating saw.

invisible edging

Plastic and metal edgings hold pavers securely in place without drawing attention to themselves. Once backfilled, they can be completely covered. Install these edgings after the excavation is completed and the gravel, but not the sand, is laid and tamped. See pages 80–81 for how to lay and screed sand for this type of installation.

Because the edging will rest on top of the gravel, take special care that the gravel is even and at the correct height. You may choose to lay landscaping fabric over the gravel before installing the edging (see page 82).

Many "landscaping" edgings are designed only to hold back mulch; they are not strong enough for a patio. Look for thick-gauge plastic or metal; typically, 12-inch spikes are driven every foot or so to anchor a true patio edging.

1 Lay and Align the Edging
Use rigid edging for straight runs and notched edging for curves. The edging height does not have to be precise, but it should not be more than ½ inch too high or too low. You may need to add or to remove gravel to maintain the correct height.

2 Pound the Spikes
Along straight runs, drive stakes through the edging's holes every foot or so—more often if the ground is soft and the spikes are easy to drive. At a curve, drive a spike into every available hole.

3 Backfill with Sod
Once the patio is laid, fill in behind the edging with strips of excavated sod that come right up to the pavers.

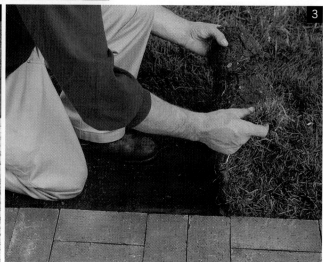

timber edging

If you are lucky, you can find railroad ties or other massive, weather-beaten pieces to use as edging. However, pressure-treated 4 × 4, 4 × 6, or 6 × 6 lumber will do nicely and turn an attractive gray in a year or two. Take care to select timbers that are straight; there is no way to unbend them. Excavate deep enough to accommodate several inches of gravel under the timbers.

1 Cut and Position the Timbers

To cut a 4 × 4 or a 4 × 6, use a small square to draw lines around all four sides. Set the blade of a 7¼-inch circular saw to full depth and check that it is square to the saw's base. Cut the two opposite sides. Cut a 6 × 6 on all four sides, then cut the middle with a hand-saw or a reciprocating saw. Set the timbers in a bed of gravel and check for the correct height and alignment. You may need to remove the timber, add or shovel away some gravel, and try again.

2 Drill Holes

You can anchor the timbers with either ½-inch concrete reinforcing bar ("rebar") or ½-inch galvanized pipe; either will rust attractively in a year or so. Equip a drill with an extra long spade bit, as wide as the anchors you will use. Drill holes through the center of the timber every 2 feet or so. If the drill or bit starts to get hot, give it a rest.

3 Drive Anchors

Use a hacksaw or a reciprocating saw equipped with a metal-cutting blade to cut two lengths of rebar or pipe to 3 feet. Use a sledgehammer to pound an anchor down through the timber and into the ground until the top of the metal is flush with the timber. If the pounding is easy, cut longer pieces; if it is difficult, cut shorter pieces. Drive anchors through all the holes.

brick or concrete-paver edging

Upright paver edging is often made of the same material as the rest of the patio, but you can choose a contrasting material instead. Soil and sod hold the edging in place. If your soil is sandy or soft, consider installing paver-on-concrete edging (see page 73). Or, set the soldiers in several inches of mortar, as shown for the sailors on the opposite page.

INSTALLING SOLDIERS

Soldiers stand upright with their edges (not their faces) facing the patio. This arrangement uses more materials to make an edging than does using sailors, which face the other way, but it is stronger.

1 Screed the Base

Stretch a guide string that is at the level of the patio surface. Dig a trench 4 inches deeper than the height of the pavers. Shovel in 3 inches of gravel and tamp firm with a hand tamper or with a piece of 4 × 4. Make a screed guide as shown from a 2 × 6 and a 2 × 4;

the 2 × 6 should extend below the 2 × 4 by the length of a soldier. Pour damp sand over the gravel. Scrape across the sand with the guide. Spray the sand with a fine mist of water, add a little more sand, and screed again.

2 Set the Bricks
Position each paver so its outside corner is about 1/8 inch away from the guide line. After you have installed 4 feet or so, lay a straight board on top and tap to achieve a smooth, even surface.

3 Tamp Firm
Use a 2 × 4 to gently tamp soil on the patio side. If the bricks go out of alignment and need to be nudged back toward the patio side, use the edge of a piece of plywood to tamp the soil into the space between the sod and the soldiers.

TILTED SAILORS

This edging adds charm to a patio, but is not as stable as soldiers. Here the sailors are being set in mortar, for extra strength, though they could be installed with tamped soil only. Tilted sailors (or soldiers) could extend upward above the patio surface, but that can create a tripping hazard. The other option is to have their uppermost corners at the same height as the patio.

Stake a straight 2 × 4 along the outer edge of the patio at the exact same height as the top of the sailors. Check with a mason's line to make sure the top is straight and test that it is either level or correctly sloped. Dig a trench 4 inches deeper than the sailors will extend downward. Working in sections 3 to 4 feet at a time, shovel 2 to 3 inches of mortar into the trench and set the sailors, tilted at the desired angle, so that one top corner is flush with the top of the 2 × 4. A quick way to maintain a consistent angle is to install sailors so that the other top corner is flush with the bottom of the 2 × 4.

TURNING A CURVE

Install benderboard edging (page 67) as a guide for a curved section. The joints between the pavers will be wider on the outside of the curve.

poured concrete edging

This is the strongest edging and will last for a long time. Unlike pouring a concrete slab, installation is not difficult and calls for no special skills.

Concrete edging need not look industrial. Concrete may be tinted or given a decorative finish when it is poured; cured concrete can be acid-stained to almost any color (see pages 116–23). Or, cover the concrete with tile, flagstone, or brick (see pages 75, 124–27). For basic instructions on building forms, mixing concrete, and finishing, see pages 104–15.

1 Build the Forms

The edging should be at least 6 inches wide and 4 inches deep; anything less massive is likely to crack. If you will cover the edging with tiles or pavers, make the edging an appropriate width.

Dig a trench wide enough to accommodate the edging plus the width of the framing boards. Shovel 3 inches of compactible gravel at the bottom, and use a 2 × 4 or 4 × 4 to tamp it firm.

Build straight forms using 2 × 4s held in place with 1 × 2 or 2 × 2 stakes; build curved forms using benderboard. Check that the forms are at the right height, and are either level or correctly sloped. Place lengths of ⅜-inch rebar down the middle of the form, held in place with rebar bolsters or with chunks of stone.

2 Pour and Screed the Concrete

Purchase bags of "high-early" or fiber-reinforced concrete. Mix batches of concrete in a wheelbarrow. Shovel the concrete into the forms. Poke with a piece of rebar all along the forms to ensure that there are no air bubbles. Screed the top by scraping in a sawing motion with a scrap of lumber.

3 Trowel the Top

Use a magnesium or wood float to further smooth the top surface and use an edging tool at the corners. Once the concrete has started to harden, remove the forms. If the outside edge will be exposed, float it as well. For a finished appearance, work the surface with a steel trowel or brush it with a broom.

The slower the concrete cures, the stronger it will be. Cover it with plastic and/or spray it with water regularly for the next four or five days.

paver-on-concrete edging

Pavers of any sort, as well as flagstones or even small boulders, can be laid on or in concrete edging. The easiest but most time-consuming method is to allow the concrete edging to cure and then to set pavers in mortar. Setting pavers directly in poured concrete saves time but calls for some skill.

MORTARING ONTO CURED CONCRETE

Pour concrete edging (opposite page) with its top lower than the patio by the thickness of the pavers you will install. Set the pavers in a dry run on the concrete and make any necessary cuts. Then set the pavers off to the side. In the example shown, bricks and stones are combined. You may choose to butt the pavers tightly together or to leave ⅜-inch gaps between them, which you will fill with mortar (see page 125).

In a wheelbarrow or container, combine a bag of mortar mix with a shovel of Portland cement, and mix with water. Use a brick trowel to spread mortar onto the concrete (see pages 140–41). Set the pavers in the mortar, their edges flush with the inside edge of the concrete. (If an uneven stone protrudes into the patio area, you will have to cut pavers to fit around it.)

SETTING IN WET CONCRETE

Build a form for concrete edging (opposite page, step 1), but use 2 × 6s instead of 2 × 4s. The form should be just wide enough to accommodate the pavers. On the inside of each form board, snap a chalk line at a paver's thickness below the top, minus ½ inch.

Mix a batch of concrete that is fortified with extra Portland cement. Pour it into the form almost up to the chalk line. Use a scrap of wood to roughly level the concrete. Set pavers in the wet concrete, using spacers to keep them ⅜ inch apart. Gently tap each paver so that it settles flush with the top of the form boards. You may need to raise or to lower the level of concrete to accomplish this. After the concrete has hardened, fill the joints with mortar (see page 125).

73

decorative edgings

Almost any material that can be solidly embedded in the ground can serve as edging. Wood rounds, logs, or upright pieces produce a woodsy effect. A short wall or a raised bed can perform double duty as an edging.

Edging that is uneven in shape is not a problem for a loose-material path or patio. You can build a paver patio first, using invisible edging (page 68), and then add the decorative edging. Many decorative edgings make it difficult to mow the lawn; they work best next to flowers or shrubs.

CLAY TILES

The terra-cotta color and texture of clay roofing tiles contrasts handsomely with both plants and stone. The tiles are not strong and can be easily cracked during installation. However, they will form a durable edging if they are firmly embedded in well-packed soil. Carefully pack and tamp soil or sand on either side. Fill the spaces between the tiles with sand.

BOULDERS

Small boulders can be set simply in shallow holes. If you will install pavers (rather than loose materials), purchase semidressed stone with at least one flat side. By chiseling away rough edges and experimenting with different configurations, you can achieve an inside edge that is fairly even.

TILE

Be sure to use floor tiles (not wall tiles) rated for outdoor use in your area. To create a slip-resistant surface, use unglazed tiles, such as quarry tiles, or install mosaic tiles—the grout lines will provide traction. The outside edge of the tiles will likely be visible.

Many tiles can be cut with a simple snap cutter, but some types require a wet saw; ask your tile dealer. Install concrete edging (page 72) and allow it to cure. Mix and spread latex-reinforced thinset mortar, using a square-notched trowel. Set the tiles in the mortar and use plastic spacers to maintain consistent grout joints. Wait overnight for the thinset to harden; then fill the joints with grout (see page 129).

SHORT-WALL EDGING

A short wall on the edge of a patio or on either side of a path clearly and attractively divides the masonry from foliage. Plants can grow at will without encroaching on the patio or path.

If you leave a 1-inch space between the wall and the pavers, rainwater can run down through the joint. If the wall and the patio are tightly abutted and the joints are filled with mortar, be sure that rainwater can easily run away from or alongside the wall.

Build short-wall edging as you would any masonry wall; see chapter four for options.

cutting and handling concrete pavers, bricks, and stone

Unless the job is small or you own a heavy-duty truck, it is probably worth the extra expense to have masonry materials delivered to the site. Discuss details of the delivery when you make the purchase. Arranging for delivery right next to the job can save you plenty of heavy lifting. Be aware that a heavy pallet may crack a driveway, especially if the truck driver drops the pallet rather than lowers it slowly.

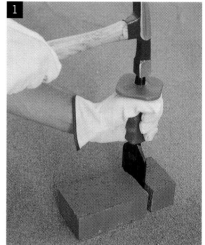

CUTTING THE OLD-FASHIONED WAY

Bricks for a wall do not have to be cut precisely, so bricklayers usually cut by hand. But patio bricks usually need to be cut with precision, and concrete pavers are virtually impossible to cut by hand. Rent a masonry saw to make straight, accurate cuts (see pages 78–79).

Common bricks made for building walls can be easily cut; pros often simply hack them in two using a brick trowel. Paving bricks are much harder and require a hammer and a brickset chisel to cut. Chips will fly—wear gloves and protective goggles.

1 Score and Break

Place the brick on a flat, resilient surface, such as a bed of sand. Press a brickset chisel firmly in place and tap with a hammer to score a line on all four sides. Hold the brickset against a score line, with its bevel (the angled side of the tip) facing the waste side of the cut. Whack the brickset hard, and the brick will break. If the break occurs in an unexpected place, just throw the brick out and try another.

2 Clean the Cut Edge

Chip or scrape away any protrusions along the cut edge, using a brick trowel or the sharp side of a brick hammer.

CUTTING A FLAGSTONE Some types of flagstone break apart with just a tap or two, while others call for a stronger effort. Cutting flagstone is an unpredictable process; don't be surprised if only half of your cuts follow the line you had in mind. Use a brickset or narrow cold chisel to score a line on both sides of the stone. Position the

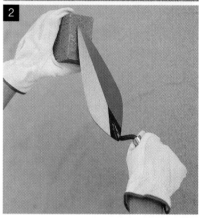

stone with the scored line on top of a scrap of wood or a pipe. Using a sledgehammer, hit the stone on the waste side to break it off.

USING A BRICK SPLITTER

A brick splitter makes fairly accurate cuts quickly and can usually be rented for a modest price. Mark the cutline and align it with the splitter's blade. Or, use the splitter's ruler to measure for the cut. Make sure that the brick is pressed snugly against the guide. Push down forcefully on the handle to break the brick.

CIRCULAR SAW CUTS

If you have 15 or fewer bricks or pavers that need precise cuts, consider using a circular saw equipped with a masonry cutting blade. Be aware, however, that the dust created by cutting masonry can eventually damage a circular saw, especially if the saw is an inexpensive model. If you feel the saw heating up, take a break to allow the motor to cool.

Attach a scrap piece of wood to the working surface, to keep the bricks from sliding as you cut. Clamp several bricks together to cut them all to the same length. For most bricks, set the blade to a depth of about ½ inch; for paving bricks and concrete pavers, set the depth to about ¼ inch. Press the saw firmly down on the pavers as you make the cut. Lower the blade and make a second pass. Repeat, until you cut most of the way through. Then break off the waste with a hammer and a chisel or finish the cut from the other side for greater precision.

To cut a concrete block, use a circular saw to score a line about ½ inch deep on each side and finish the cut with a cold chisel and a sledgehammer.

WET SAW TECHNIQUES

Buying an inexpensive wet saw will save you the hassle of running to the rental store every time you want to cut masonry or certain types of tile. However, an inexpensive saw will cut more slowly and may not be as accurate as a rental saw; also, its blade may become dull after cutting 30 concrete pavers or so.

If you rent a wet-cutting masonry saw, also called a tub saw, obtain complete instructions. Test the saw to make sure that the tray glides smoothly and is square to the blade. Check that you have all the guides you need for making any angle cuts.

Water must spray onto the blade constantly; even a few seconds of dry cutting can dull a blade. On some wet saws, the pump must be placed in a 5-gallon bucket filled with water. When the bucket runs out of water, refill it by opening a drain hole in the pan of the saw. On other models the pump is placed in the pan, so there is rarely a need to refill. However, the blade will last longer if you regularly throw out dirty water and replace with clean water.

STRAIGHT CUT To make a basic cut, place the paver in the tray and hold it against the back guide so that it's square to the blade. Turn on the saw and check that water flows to the blade. Slide the tray forward slowly to slice through the paver.

ANGLE CUT Typical guides hold the paver at 45 degrees and other specified angles; an adjustable angle guide is also available. Hold the paver firmly against the attachment as you slide the paver forward to make the cut.

CUTOUT Make two cuts for a cutout (or notch). Tilt the paver up to avoid overcutting the top of the paver; the bottom of the cut must be slightly longer than the top. Hold the paver against the back guide to ensure a square cut.

STRAIGHT CUT

ANGLE CUT

CUTOUT

CURVE CUT Take your time when cutting a curve. Hold the paver firmly with both hands and tilt it up, so that the bottom of the cut will be slightly deeper than the top. Press the paver gently against the blade and move it from side to side, removing only a small amount of the paver at a time.

MEASURING FOR ANGLE CUTS

On a patio where pavers must be cut precisely, install all the full-size pavers first, then measure for cutting the fill-in pieces. This makes it easier to achieve tight fits. Also, it allows you to rent the saw only for the time when you actually need it.

Rather than measuring, you will usually get a tighter fit if you hold the paver in place and mark it for a cut (below left). Mark for both sides of the cut, then draw a straight line between the marks. To ensure that you are getting the angle right, use a T bevel (below). Hold it in place as shown, then tighten the wing nut to preserve the angle.

CARRYING PAVERS

Wear gloves most of the time when handling pavers. (The exception is when cutting; gloves may catch on a saw blade.) Rather than stacking and carrying a pile of bricks, use a pair of brick tongs, also called a hod carrier.

screeding for a patio with invisible or uneven edging

If your patio has solid edging that matches the height of the patio, use the method shown on pages 82–83 to screed the sand. If your patio lacks such a consistent guide along its perimeter, use pipes as screed guides, as shown on these pages.

Start by laying out, excavating, and spreading gravel (see pages 58–63). Depending on local soil conditions, you may choose first to lay landscaping fabric (see page 82) and then to lay the pipes on top of the fabric. Check with a contractor or with your building department to see what they recommend.

1 Lay and Check Screed Pipes
You can use copper or galvanized pipe as guides, but plastic pipe is inexpensive and light. For a 1-inch-thick layer of sand, use ¾-inch pipe (which has an outside diameter of about 1 inch); for a 1½-inch-thick layer, use 1-inch pipe. Space the pipes about 6 feet apart; pipes parallel to edging should be about a foot away from the edging. Cut pieces to fit within an inch or so. Lay a long, straight board across several pipes to make sure that they describe a fairly even surface. Check that the patio will be level and parallel to the house and sloped down and away from the house at a rate of about ¼ inch per foot. Adjust a pipe up or down by adding or removing gravel under it.

2 Spread Sand
Pour sand into the area and roughly smooth it with a garden rake so that it is slightly higher than the pipes at most points.

3 Wet the Sand

If the sand is not already moist, spray it with a garden hose set on mist, until it is damp.

4 Tamp

Use a power tamper to press the sand firmly into place. If there are any footprints or low spots in the sand, fill them in.

5 Screed the Sand

Lay a straight 2 × 4 across two or three of the pipes. Press the board onto the pipes and pull or push it across the patio to produce a smooth surface. Fill in any low spots, moisten, and repeat.

6 Remove Pipes and Fill Voids

Remove the pipes without disturbing the surface. Fill the voids with sand and pat the surface smooth with a scrap of wood.

screeding for a patio with solid edging

Once the site has been laid out, excavated, edged, and filled with well-tamped gravel (see pages 58–63), you're ready for the final substrate element, a layer of sand. If you do not have edging that is solid and at the same height as the patio surface, use the technique shown on pages 80–81.

Local codes may specify 1 or 2 inches of sand. Use a long board and a tape measure to check the average depth of the gravel below the edging; power-tamping may have compacted it,

so you may need a little more sand than you had originally planned. Sweeping the patio will be easier if the pavers end up about ¼ inch above the edging.

Arrange for the sand to be delivered directly into the patio, if possible. In addition to coarse sand made for underlayment, you will need bags of fine sand or stone dust to fill the joints between the pavers.

1 Spread Landscaping Fabric

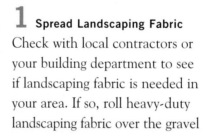

Check with local contractors or your building department to see if landscaping fabric is needed in your area. If so, roll heavy-duty landscaping fabric over the gravel

base. Work to eliminate any folds. Cut the pieces accurately and butt them tightly against the edging—where weeds are most likely to grow. Overlap parallel strips by 6 to 8 inches. Hold the sheets in place with small mounds of sand to keep them from blowing away.

2 Install a Temporary Screed Guide

If your patio is less than 10 feet wide, skip this step. For a larger patio, cut a 2 × 4 to fit, and attach it 6 to 10 feet away from the edging so that its top is at exactly the same height as the edging to which it runs parallel. Screw the 2 × 4 to the edging or to the house, at both ends. Every 3 or 4 feet, drive a 2 × 4 stake against the temporary screed guide outside the area to be screeded (see step 5) and about an inch below the top of the 2 × 4. Double-check that the temporary screed is at the correct height all along its length.

3 Make a Screed

Start with a straight 2 × 4 or 2 × 6 that is about 2 feet longer than the area to be screeded. Cut one or more strips of plywood to the thickness of the pavers plus the width of the 2 × 4 or 2 × 6. The plywood should be about 4 inches shorter than the distance between the edging pieces. Attach the plywood with screws as shown. The plywood should extend below the board by the thickness of a paver—minus ¼ inch, if you want the pavers to be ¼ inch above the edging.

4 Spread Sand

Taking care not to disturb the landscaping fabric or the gravel, spread the sand with a square shovel and a rake until it is slightly higher than its final level. (see step 5). The sand should be a little damp; if at any point it dries out, spray it with a hose nozzle set on mist. Power-tamp the sand (see page 81, step 4) and spread more sand to fill in any low spots. Moisten the sand if it dries out.

5 Screed the Sand

If the screed is longer than 6 feet, do this step with a helper. Starting at one end, move the screed across the patio to smooth the sand. Set a paver on top of the sand to see that the sand is at the correct height. It may help to saw back and forth as you push or pull the screed across the sand. Fill any voids, moisten the sand if necessary, and repeat until you achieve a perfectly smooth surface.

6 Stretch a Guide Line

To prepare for laying pavers, stretch a length of mason's line across the patio to act as a height guide. Pull the line taut, so that it does not sag in the middle. Attach it with a nail or a screw, or wrap it around a temporary stake, as shown.

paver patterns

Don't compromise when it comes to the paver pattern. Laying the pattern you want most may take only half a day more than laying a simple pattern—a small investment compared with all that work you put in excavating and laying a bed of gravel and sand. In addition to the patterns shown here, consider the circular patterns shown on page 90.

"Interlocking" pavers have shapes that automatically make patterns (see page 34). However, it is not difficult to create a richly textured surface using rectangular units. Rectangular or square pavers create just as strong a surface, as long as their joints are filled with fine sand.

MODULAR PAVER PATTERNS

To make the patterns shown at right, the pavers must be factory-produced to precise dimensions, and they must be modular—half as wide as they are long. If you rent a wet masonry saw and allow yourself half a day or so for cutting, you can make any of the traditional patterns.

Jack-on-jack is the easiest to install, but only by a small margin. Half-basketweave and basketweave (with or without the 2 × 4 grid) are nearly as easy. None of these patterns requires a lot of cutting; if you arrange to move two sides of the edging after the pavers are installed, you can sometimes get away with no cuts at all.

For the pinwheel pattern, every fifth paver must be half-sized. The running bond and 90-degree herringbone patterns also call for plenty of half-sized pavers. If half-sized pavers are not available precut, you can mass-produce them using a wet masonry saw.

The 45-degree herringbone pattern requires lots of 45-degree cuts of various sizes. When installing a running bond, start by cutting plenty of half pavers; you'll need them for every other paver along one side.

A patio can be divided into a grid of squares or rectangles using 2 × 4s. The sections can be filled with pavers in most any pattern.

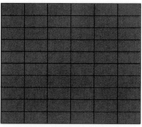

JACK-ON-JACK

45-DEGREE HERRINGBONE

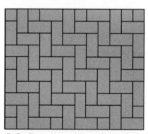

90-DEGREE HERRINGBONE

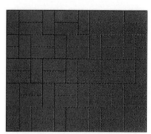

HALF-BASKETWEAVE

RUNNING BOND

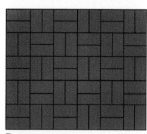

BASKETWEAVE

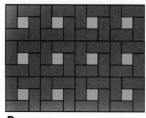

PINWHEEL

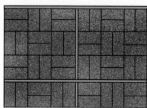

**BASKETWEAVE
WITH 2 × 4 GRID**

CONCRETE PAVER ENSEMBLES

Many companies sell pavers in "mixed pallets," which contain pavers in as many as six different sizes and shapes. These make a complicated-looking pattern, but in reality the pieces can be assembled more or less randomly. Sort the pavers first, so that you can distribute the various sizes more or less equally.

In addition, some large pavers have inscribed patterns that look like several small pavers butted together. This speeds up installation, but these pavers are fairly heavy, so you may need help.

Many concrete pavers come in pallets that include pavers of several different colors, for an overall variegated appearance. You may need to shuffle the pavers so you don't end up with a preponderance of one color in any area.

STONE DUST TO FILL JOINTS

Usually, the joints of a dry-laid paver patio are filled with fine sand (page 87, step 6), which has a neutral color that blends with most paver colors. For a more geometric look, spend a little more for dark-colored stone dust, which is finer than the sand.

setting pavers

On these two pages you'll see how to install pavers in a 90-degree herringbone pattern. For other patterns and installation possibilities, look through pages 84–85 and 88–93.

As long as the sand was screeded correctly (pages 80–83), the pavers you set will be at the correct height. However, it is a good idea to stretch a length of mason's line from edging to edging to double-check. If the patio level is too high or low, you may need to screed again.

1 Start Laying Pavers

Start in one corner and set several pavers to abut the edging. Use a level or a straightedge to check that the pavers are at the desired height; if they are not, adjust the screed and screed again. Set each paver straight down onto the bed, gently scraping the side of the edging or an already-laid paver as you lower it; if you slide a paver more than ¼ inch or so, you will create waves in the sand and the surface will not be level. Install all pavers so that they fit snugly against each other.

2 Tap with a Beater Board

After 10 or 12 pavers have been set, place a beater board—a flat 2 × 4 or 2 × 6 about 2 feet long—on top and tap with a hammer or a rubber mallet. If a paver is noticeably higher than its neighbor, tap it directly with the mallet.

3 Continue Laying Pavers

As you install more pavers across the surface, move the guide string with you every 2 feet or so. If you need to kneel on top of the patio, first lay down a piece of plywood large enough to support your toes, as well as your knees, to evenly distribute your weight. Bricks can be pushed out of position until they all are locked in by the edging.

4 Screed the Other Side of a Temporary Guide

If you installed a temporary screed guide, remove it once you have finished with one section. Spread sand in the next section. Rest the screed on the patio surface at one end and the edging on the other side, screed the sand, and continue laying pavers.

5 Move Edging to Minimize Cutting

You may be able to avoid cutting pavers at one edge of the patio by adjusting the edging. Install pavers up to the end of the patio; then move the edging to abut them. In the case of 2-by edging (as shown), push the edging up against the pavers and drive stakes and screws to secure it.

6 Sweep Fine Sand into the Joints

Scatter very fine sand over the pavers and use a soft-bristled broom to sweep the sand into the joints. If the sand is wet, allow it to dry and sweep again.

7 Power Tamp or Spray

Run a vibrating plate compactor over the surface, which will cause the fine sand to settle down into the joints. Sweep more sand into the joints and tamp again. Alternatively, moisten the patio by spraying it with a mist of water; this also will cause the sand to settle.

FORTY-FIVE-DEGREE HERRINGBONE PATTERN

Just before you screed the sand for the last time, measure and mark the exact center of the edging on two parallel sides of the patio. Measure to double-check that the two marks are equidistant from the corners. Tack a small nail at one of the marks (usually, where the patio abuts the house) and hook the clip of a chalk line to the nail. Unroll the chalk line and put it out of the way, taking care not to jostle the chalk. Finish screeding. Pull the chalk line taut between the two marks and snap a line in the sand.

Install the first pavers with painstaking precision; if they are slightly out of alignment, the problem will magnify itself over the length of the patio. The pavers' corners should just touch the chalk line, as shown. Use an angle square to check that the pavers are 45 degrees to the line. Carefully install a V-shaped row of pavers along the line for about 6 feet; after that, it will be impossible to change the alignment, so ignore the line and just install pavers tight against each other.

If the edging and paver installation is very accurate, you will end up with a large number of cuts that are exactly 45 degrees. However, it is likely that things will move slightly out of alignment, so ask for an adjustable saw guide, which will enable you to tinker with the cutting angles.

OTHER PATTERNS

Installing a basketweave, a half-basketweave, or a pinwheel pattern (shown below) isn't difficult, as long as you pay close attention. Every 15 minutes or so, stand back and examine the installation to make sure you didn't make any mistakes.

The half-pavers in a pinwheel pattern can be of a different material, as long as they are the right size. They must be the same thickness and must not be larger than the width of the other pavers; it's all right if they are slightly smaller.

LAYING PAVERS IN A FRAMED GRID

For this installation it's essential that each framed section of the grid be perfectly square (or rectangular). Each section should be sized to hold only full-sized pavers, so that no paver cutting is required.

Estimate the overall size of the patio, and excavate the area a little larger than needed. Install wood or timber edging on two adjacent sides. Each edging piece should be longer than needed; you will cut them to length when you near completion of the patio. Lay a bed of well-tamped gravel, 4 inches below the top of the edging.

For the grid framing, use 2 × 4s made of pressure-treated or other rot-resistant lumber. When measuring for the grid, lay pavers in dry runs, and add ¼-inch plywood spacers as shown, to make certain that the pavers will fit. First install a series of 2 × 4s that run the entire length of the patio, then install short boards between them. Fasten the boards by drilling pilot holes and angle-driving 2½-inch deck screws. Finish the framing by cutting the two edging pieces to fit and filling in with the two remaining pieces.

When the grid is finished, pour and screed sand in each section, using a short screed guide. Lay the pavers in the pattern of your choice.

CUTTING IN PLACE

If you want to install a border along one edge or around the perimeter of a patio, you must cut the pavers in a straight line. You could snap a chalk line and then cut each paver individually, but the resulting line may not be as even as you'd like. Another option is to rent a gas-powered masonry cutoff saw and cut the line in one fell swoop. Obtain thorough instructions from the rental staff and practice on scrap pieces before you make the crucial cut. It may help to anchor a straight board to use as a guide.

CIRCULAR PATTERNS

Pavers arranged in circles, fans, or winding curves add warmth and distinction to a patio. Installing these shapes requires extra planning, time, and effort, but most installations can be accomplished with no special skills.

An informal circular patio (right) can be built entirely with standard-sized pavers, though you may want a special stone or several cut stones at the very center. Sometimes you will need to adjust the positions of pavers in order to achieve consistent joint widths. Once assembled, plastic edging (page 68) can be slipped under the outermost pavers and spiked to hold the patio firmly

together. Near the center, joints may be too wide to simply fill with sand; so, mix a batch of stiff mortar and carefully shovel it in with a garden trowel or use a grout bag, as shown on page 125.

A circular section like the one shown at left calls for custom-cutting stones. To figure the angles, experiment by cutting paver-sized pieces of cardboard.

Circular or fan-shaped concrete paver ensembles make it easy; all the pieces you need are cut to the right shapes, and you simply set them like the pieces of a puzzle.

curved path

A paver path is essentially a long, narrow patio. You have the same options for edgings and paving materials, and the building techniques are much the same. This page shows setting pavers in sand. See pages 94–95 for a loose-material path.

A path with little foot traffic can be as narrow as 2 feet, but in order for two people to pass comfortably, a path should be at least 40 inches wide.

Space the edging so that you can install all full-sized pavers; it would be tedious to cut pavers all along one side. Set out a row of pavers that is the desired width of the path. Cut a 2 × 4 spacer to $\frac{1}{2}$ inch longer than the paver run (to accommodate minor discrepancies in size). Use this 2 × 4 as shown at bottom left to check the spacing between the edgings. Every 3 feet or so, position the 2 × 4 between the edgings and drive stakes on either side.

A crowned walk sheds water quickly and ensures against puddles. To make a screed for a crowned walk, cut a curve along the working edge of the tool. At its ends, the plywood edge should extend down below the handle by the thickness of a paver; at the highest point, in the middle, it should be 1 to $1\frac{1}{2}$ inches higher. Screed the sand and install the pavers as you would for a patio. If you end up with a gap of $\frac{1}{2}$ inch or less between paver and edging, just fill it with fine sand.

large pavers with wide joints

Large adobe blocks, concrete steppers, and even chunks of used concrete can be set with joints that are ³⁄₄ to 2 inches wide, allowing ample room for crevice plants. (You can also install bricks and small pavers with joints up to ³⁄₄ inch wide. However, wider joints may make the installation look sloppy rather than charming.)

Joints can be filled with fine compactible gravel (see page 127) or with rough sand. Alternatively, you can fill the joints with soil and plants. The larger the paving units, the more crevice plants can spread.

Pavers set far apart may develop wobbles over time and need to be reset, especially if the crevice plants have strong roots.

1 Install the Edging and Plan the Layout

Excavate and install a gravel bed as if for a standard patio (see pages 58–63). Usually it looks best to enclose such a patio with either invisible edging or massive timbers; narrow edging will look out of place. Lay the pavers in a dry run with the desired joints. If the patio must fit in a defined space and you do not want to cut the pavers to fit, adjust the joint widths so that they come out even. If the pavers are factory-made to precise sizes, use spacers, such as scraps of 2 × 4 or ⁵⁄₄ decking (which is 1 inch thick). If they are irregular in shape, place a group of them forming a square of 3 to 4 feet, spaced as you desire.

Measure to find the center points of the joints that occur on the outside of each square. Mark each center point, so you can string layout lines when you install the pavers. Remove the pavers, add sand, and screed (see pages 82–83).

2 Place Pavers in a Grid

Tack small nails at each of the marks you made in step 1 and stretch mason's line to form a grid. (If you cannot drive nails into the edging, use stakes or weights to hold the lines.) Double-check that all the squares are the same size. Place pavers to fill a grid and fine-tune the placement to achieve joints that are relatively consistent in width. If you need to move a paver, pick it up and set it back down rather than sliding it. Use a straight board to check that the pavers are even with each other. If a paver is wobbly, pick it up and add or remove sand underneath.

3 Fill the Joints

Use a square shovel or a garden trowel to fill the joints with soil that is appropriate for the crevice plants you have chosen (see pages 42–43). Because this soil gets tightly compacted, often it is best to mix some sand in with potting soil to produce a soil that is firm but able to drain.

4 Tamp the Soil

Sweep the surface, using light broom strokes. Gently tamp the joints, using a board that is slightly thinner than the joints. Fill and sweep again. Sow seeds or add plants to the joints if you wish (see pages 42–43).

installing loose materials

This is the easiest way to install a path or patio. Excavation is not as deep as for a paver patio; edging does not have to be precisely spaced; and installing the surface is simply a matter of spreading and compressing. However, the job must be done right. Install edging at the correct height, so that it effectively contains the loose material while being low enough for the lawn mower to pass over. Materials must be firmly tamped, to keep them from scattering.

A loose-material surface is ideal if nearby trees have sent roots near the surface. Rainwater can easily percolate through the surface, and if the roots cause waves, you can just rake the surface smooth.

A surface made with pebbles or large-size gravel is easily scattered and may make for loose footing; bicycles and wheelbarrows have trouble with such surfaces and may do a bit of damage. However, loose materials drain well and make a nice crunchy sound when walked upon. A surface made with tiny stones, such as crushed rock or decomposed granite, can form a surface that is surprisingly hard and stable once compacted. Ask your supplier how various materials perform in your area.

LAYING A PATH

Excavate to a depth of 4 inches, install edging, and tamp the ground firm. If it is recommended in your area, cover the soil with a layer of landscaping fabric.

1 Lay a Gravel Base
Shovel and rake a 2-inch layer of compactible gravel, and spray it with a fine mist until it is thoroughly moist.

2 Compress the Base
You can use a vibrating plate compactor to compress the base, but a drum roller may be easier to navigate on a narrow path. The base must be firmly compressed so that less attractive stones will not work their way up through the finished surface.

3 Spread and Rake the Top Coat
Use a rake to spread the finish material, taking care not to disturb the base coat. If the material is small-grained, tamp it; do not attempt to tamp large pebbles or stones.

PATH WITH STEPPINGSTONES

Flagstones or other steppingstones can be set amid a gravel path. Excavate, install edging, and lay a bed of well-tamped gravel, a steppingstone's thickness below the top of the edging. To set each stone, first pour a small amount of rough sand on the gravel and work to produce a stone that does not wobble (see page 53). Once the stones are all in place, use a rake to spread the gravel around the stones, to within $\frac{1}{2}$ inch of the top of the edging. Spray with a mist of water and spread more gravel if needed.

LOOSE MATERIALS AROUND A TREE

At a bare minimum, keep solid paving at least 2 feet away from tree trunks, the paving could cause the trees to die of thirst. Before paving around a tree, it's best to consult with a nursery to determine how fast the tree will grow, how much water it needs, and how close to the surface the roots will grow. If you encounter large roots when excavating, be aware that cutting them could cause part or all of the tree to die.

When installing a patio near a tree, install edging to form a box around the trunk and install pavers up to the edging. Fill the inside of the box with large, attractive pebbles or rocks.

mixed-material paths and patios

Create a crazy-quilt pattern using just about any material that can survive in the ground. Take your time to develop a look that suits your yard and expresses your personality. Often, a few subtle rearrangements can transform a sloppy hodgepodge into an artistic arrangement.

Though the surface may be rustic, the edging and subsurface will need to be as substantial as those of a standard paver patio or walk. Follow the methods described on pages 60–83.

Here we show a dry-laid path, which is appropriate as long as you are installing elements that are likely to stay in place. Less stable materials should be mortared onto a concrete slab. The techniques used for pebble mosaics, on pages 130–31, may also be useful.

1 Install Edging and Gravel
Excavate, install edging, and install a 3-inch bed of well-tamped compactible gravel. If you will install pavers or stones with tight joints, add and screed a 1½-inch-thick layer of sand. The edging should be about ½ inch higher than the thickest timber or stone that will be installed. Lay timbers across the edging, experimenting until you find the arrangement that you like best. Mark both sides of each timber where it crosses the edging. Use a square to extend both marks straight up; then use a square to mark the cutting angle across the top and bottom.

2 Cut the Timbers

If you are experienced in the use of a chain saw, you can quickly cut through timbers; the cuts will not be precise. Alternatively, set a circular saw's blade to maximum depth and cut along each line. If needed, finish cutting the inside of the timber, using a handsaw or a reciprocating saw. Set the timbers in place. Add sand as needed to provide a stable base for each timber.

3 Add Large Stones

Between the timbers fill with compactible gravel just high enough to support the larger stones at the same height as the timbers and edging. Push a stone firmly into the gravel, then remove it and spread a small bed of coarse sand. Set the stone in the sand. If the stone wobbles, tilt it up and add, or scrape away, sand as needed.

4 Fill with Pebbles and Medium-Sized Stones

Shovel pebbles or gravel into the spaces around the large stones and spread pebbles around with a rake. Embed medium-sized stones among the pebbles. If the overall surface is fairly level, use a power tamper or a roller (see pages 62 and 94). Otherwise, walk over the entire surface and tamp with a heavy board or a hand tamper to make sure each element is wobble-free.

planning stairs

If you have a gentle slope, or if you need only a couple of steps in a rustic setting, stair construction can be casual. For example, you could excavate and position large stone slabs. If a step is too high or too low, you probably can fix the problem by removing or adding soil to the area above or below the step.

However, for a stairway of three or more steps to be comfortable to walk on, all the steps must have the same rise (the height of the step) and run (the length of the tread). Inconsistent rises or runs will make a stairway a tripping hazard.

Steps should be at least 2 feet wide; 3 feet is a common width, and 4 feet will allow people to walk abreast. Spacious stairs make a pleasant place to sit. Unless the steps are made of porous material such as gravel, they should be slightly sloped down or to the side, so that rainwater can easily run off.

DESIGNING A STAIRWAY

To be safe to climb, a stairway needs a proper ratio of rise to run.

The run for each step plus twice the rise should equal 25 to 27 inches. For instance, if a step is 5½ inches high (the thickness of a 6 × 6), its tread should be about 15 inches deep (5½ × 2 = 11; 11 + 15 = 26). If the rise is greater, then the run must become smaller. For instance, a step with a 7-inch rise requires a run that is around 12 inches. The most common rise/run combinations are shown at bottom left.

To calculate the rise and the run on a sloped area, hold a long, straight board with a level on top and measure down from it to find the stairway's total rise. Divide the total rise by the desired rise height for each step to find out how many steps you need. Then multiply the number of steps by the run for each step to estimate the total length of the stairway.

You may need to adjust the rise or run, or even the number of steps, to make it work. Or, plan to add or to dig away the ground at the bottom.

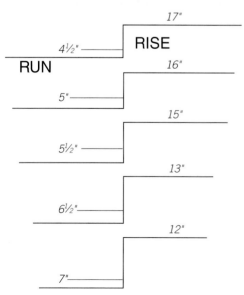

EXCAVATING

Slopes are rarely at exactly the same angle as the stairs will be. When excavating for a gravel bed under a set of stairs, chances are you will have to dig deeper in some areas than in others. As you excavate a high spot, you may be able to use the soil to fill in a low spot. An arrangement like that shown at right will help you find the correct depth of excavation for the stairway.

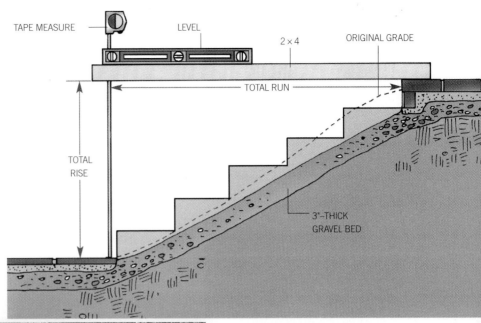

TAPE MEASURE
LEVEL
2 × 4
ORIGINAL GRADE
TOTAL RUN
TOTAL RISE
3"-THICK GRAVEL BED

LAYING ROUGH STAIRS

A stairway like the one shown at left is best built using massive slabs that are similar in thickness, so that they automatically create steps with fairly consistent riser heights. The slabs should be 5 to 8 inches thick. The front of each step rests on and overlaps the step below, so the slabs should be at least 3 inches wider than the desired run. Slabs like these are a very heavy and difficult to move.

If the soil is stable and if the excavation does not call for adding much soil (see above), steps like these simply can be set on top of the excavation. Use a square shovel to cut an opening for the bottom step and check that it is level in both directions. Set the slab in place, then excavate and lay each succeeding step in rising order. Excavate carefully, so that the slabs rest on undisturbed soil.

building stairs

This stairway is basically a series of small patios, each with timber edging and bricks or pavers set in a gravel-and-sand bed. A 4 × 6 set on edge is 5½ inches tall—a good height for a step rise.

See page 98 for planning rise and run. Of course, you cannot adjust the rises on this stairway. Plan the stairway with consistent rises starting at the top; when you reach the bottom, you can probably excavate or build up the grade to make the last step the same height as the others.

Mark off the area with mason's lines and stakes and measure as shown on page 99 to excavate the area. The initial excavation does not have to be precise; you can make adjustments as you lay the frames for the steps.

1 Build Timber Frames

Purchase 4 × 6 pressure-treated lumber; look for straight pieces that are not deeply cracked. On a flat surface, lay pavers in a dry run to determine the inside dimensions of the frame; you should not have to cut any pavers. The steps should be around 15 inches deep—including the front 4 × 6 (but not the rear 4 × 6).

Cut the timbers with a circular saw or with a 12-inch power miter saw. Working on a flat surface, assemble the pieces. At each joint, drill a pilot hole, using a long bit, and use a socket wrench to drive two 7-inch lag screws with washers.

2 Lay the First Frame in a Gravel Bed

Place 2 to 3 inches of compactible gravel at the bottom of the stairway 5½ inches below the calculated level for the first step. Tamp with a hand tamper or with a 2 × 4. Set the frame on the gravel and check that it is level or sloped in the desired direction.

3 Stack and Anchor the Timbers

Add succeeding frames one at a time, checking each for correct slope. Excavate and add gravel as needed for each frame.

Anchor each frame with at least four pieces of reinforcing bar. Whether the frame piece rests on gravel or on another 4 × 6, drill a hole and drive a piece of rebar 2 to 3 feet long, depending on soil conditions. Driving the rebar should take some effort but should not be a struggle.

4 Screed the Base

When all the frames have been installed, check that they are all stable. In each frame, pour compactible gravel up to a depth of one paver thickness plus 1½ inches below the top of the frame. Tamp the gravel with a 2 × 4. Shovel in sand and use a scrap piece of wood to screed the sand so that it is a paver-thickness below the frame.

5 Set the Pavers

Place the pavers into the frames.

Tap with a board and a rubber mallet and check with a straight board to see that they are all at the same height.

6 Fill the Joints

Sweep fine sand to fill the joints, spray with a fine mist, and repeat the process once or twice until the sand no longer sinks down when you spray it.

casting concrete

CONCRETE HAS LONG BEEN ASSOCIATED WITH DURABILITY, and for good reason. A slab that is thick enough for its purpose and that rests on a bed of firmly tamped gravel will remain stable for many decades. A properly sized footing provides rock-solid support for a wall or other structure. ■ Pouring concrete is not a job to be taken lightly; a mistake in planning can lead to a problem that is very difficult to correct. A small patio (say, 8 by 10 feet) with a broomed finish is within the reach of a skilled do-it-yourselfer, but a larger size or smoother finish will be difficult to achieve. Before pouring a slab, study pages 104–15. You may decide to contract with a pro or at least to hire some professional help. ■ Nowadays, concrete is beautiful as well as durable. A variety of methods and products make it possible to create a wide range of colors and textures while pouring new concrete. If you have an old, dreary-looking slab, there are many ways to beautify it. Some of these techniques are homeowner friendly, others are best left to the pros.

concrete basics

In most areas, you need a permit to pour more than a very small concrete slab. Check with your building department; they have very specific requirements, and you'll achieve better results if you follow them to the letter.

THE RIGHT MIX

Concrete is composed of Portland cement, sand, gravel (also called aggregate), and water. For different ways of putting the ingredients together, see pages 106–7.

Portland cement is the glue that holds it all together. The more cement, the stronger the concrete. To strengthen a small batch of concrete or mortar, add a shovel or two of cement. When ordering from a ready-mix concrete company, specify how much cement you want. A "six-bag mix" contains six bags of cement per yard of concrete—strong enough for most projects, but check with

your building inspector to make sure a stronger mix isn't required.

Gravel stones should be no larger than one-third the thickness of the slab; avoid the temptation to throw in large rocks to fill space. A correct mix will have enough sand to fill in the spaces between the gravel stones. If dirt gets into a concrete mix, the concrete will be weakened.

The mix should contain enough water so that you can easily pour and work it; but too much water weakens the concrete and causes cracks. An inspector may test concrete for "slump" using a special testing cone (below).

A sag of about 4 or 5 inches indicates the right consistency for most jobs—not too soupy and not too dry.

If you live in an area with freezing winters, order air-entrained concrete, which contains tiny bubbles. The bubbles lend a bit of flexibility, so the concrete is less likely to crack when it freezes. An air-entrained agent can be added when using a power mixer.

If it might freeze during the pour or a few days afterward, consider ordering an accelerating additive, which makes the concrete harden quicker. If the weather is hot and dry, consider adding a retardant, which slows up the drying time. If the concrete sets too fast, you may not have enough time to adequately finish the surface.

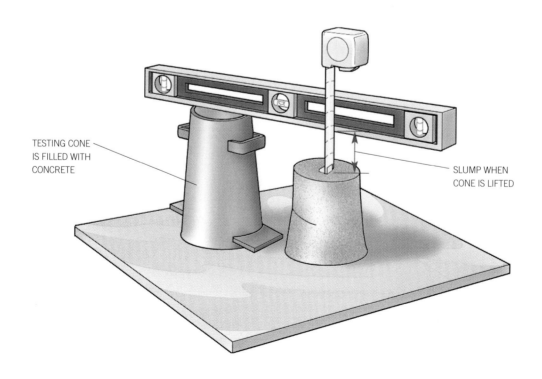

TESTING CONE IS FILLED WITH CONCRETE

SLUMP WHEN CONE IS LIFTED

REINFORCING CONCRETE

Building departments have specific requirements for steel reinforcement. Wire mesh embedded in a slab keeps the slab together if it cracks during or after curing. Reinforcing bar (rebar) is used to make walls and footings stronger. To prevent concrete from cracking while it cures, you can have fiber mesh added to the ready-mix truck, or you can buy bags of dry-mix concrete that are fiber reinforced. Unfortunately, fiber mesh does nothing after the concrete is cured, so don't make the common mistake of using it to replace wire mesh.

CALCULATING CONCRETE NEEDS

Use the following guidelines to figure gravel and sand needs as well as concrete. Take careful measurements of the area to be filled. Measure for thickness in a number of spots to obtain a reliable average; a discrepancy of $\frac{1}{2}$ inch can make a big difference in the amount of concrete you need. A supplier can quickly calculate for you, but it's a good idea for you to double-check the calculations. This is easy to do, if you use a calculator.

Concrete is typically sold by the cubic yard, also just called a yard. A yard of concrete (or sand, or gravel) fills an area 3 feet by 3 feet by 3 feet. For small projects like postholes, you may choose to measure cubic footage instead. A 60-pound bag produces $\frac{1}{2}$ cubic

foot; a 90-pound bag yields $\frac{2}{3}$ cubic foot.

For a rectangular slab or footing, multiply the width in feet times the length in feet, times the thickness in inches. Divide the result by 12 to get the number of cubic feet. Divide that number by 27 to get the number of cubic yards. For example, if a slab measures 12 feet by 14 feet and is $3\frac{1}{2}$ inches thick, use the following formula:

$12 \times 14 \times 3.5 = 588$

$588 \div 12 = 49$ cubic feet

$49 \div 27 = 1.8$ cubic yards.

Add about 10 percent for waste and order 2 yards.

To figure for a circular slab (which is actually a shallow cylinder), multiply the radius in feet squared times pi (3.14), times the thickness in inches. As with a rectangle, divide that number by 12 to get the cubic feet and divide that sum by 27 to get the number of cubic yards. For example, if an area is 8 feet in radius (16 feet in diameter) and 4 inches thick, use the following formula:

$8 \times 8 = 64$

$64 \times 3.14 \times 4 = 804$

$804 \div 12 = 67$ cubic feet

$67 \div 27 = 2.5$ cubic yards

Add about 10 percent for waste and order $2\frac{3}{4}$ yards.

If your patio is an irregular shape, divide it into rectangles and portions of circles to obtain an estimate of the square footage. In the example shown below, a patio is divided into four rectangles and two quarter circles. Note how area #2 is treated as a rectangle.

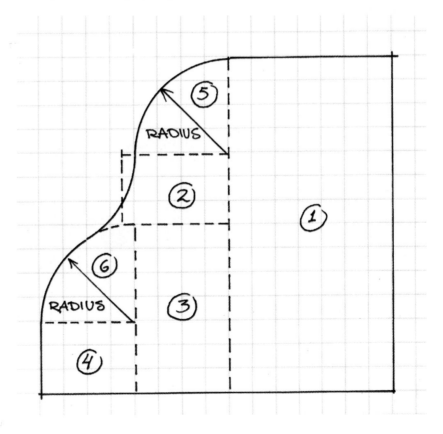

mixing concrete

Concrete must be mixed and poured without delays so that you have enough time to screed, float, and finish it (see pages 108–15). Think through the process thoroughly and plan not only how you will mix it, but also where to place the ingredients and how to transport them to the site.

MIX IT YOURSELF OR HAVE IT DELIVERED?

Ready-mix concrete (from a delivery truck) is reliable in strength and saves plenty of trouble. If you need more than ½ yard of concrete, ordering ready-mix concrete is usually worth any extra expense, even if you have to pay for a full yard. However, it will cost extra money if the truck has to wait around more than 30 minutes. If you need to pour in small batches, you may want to mix your own.

Mixing your own may have added advantages, especially if you are a beginner. If you divide a project into small sections— say, by installing permanent wood dividers (see page 109)—you can pour and then finish sections as small as 4 feet square. This will give you plenty of time to learn how to finish the concrete, and any mistakes will be small. On the other hand, if you order ready-mix and pour a 400-square-foot slab and then find yourself unable to finish it, you will have a major disaster.

If you live in a remote area, or if you want to mix concrete in small batches, consider renting an electric- or gas-powered concrete mixer and buying separate dry ingredients. This method allows you to add any special ingredients, such as colorant.

For a small project, consider dry-mix bags; fourteen 60-pound bags will yield ¼ yard. The work will be slow but won't take up as much space in your yard as would mixing dry ingredients.

MIXING BAGS

You can buy a large plastic mixing trough, but mixing in a wheelbarrow is much more convenient.

A large, heavy-duty wheelbarrow can handle two or even three 80-pound bags at a time.

Compared with the value of your time and effort, concrete is cheap. Spend a little more money for "high-early" or fiber-reinforced concrete, which is sure to be strong.

Place the wheelbarrow on a stable surface, so it won't tip over while you work. Squirt about an inch of water in the bottom of the wheelbarrow and pour in a bag or two of concrete mix. Mix using a mortar hoe; be sure to scrape the bottom and sides. Add water slowly, mixing as you go, and take care to produce the right consistency (see page 107).

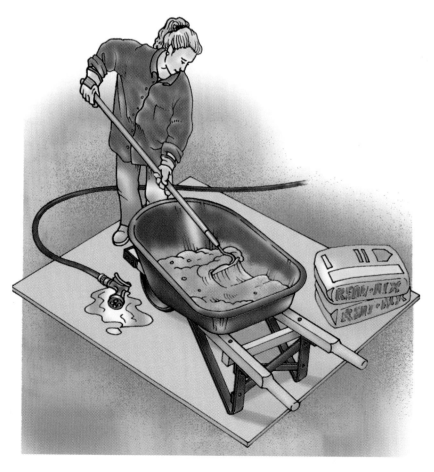

USING A POWER MIXER

Rent a mixer with a capacity of at least 4 cubic feet. A mixer can be either electric or gas-powered. Stabilize the mixer so it does not "walk" while it is mixing.

Consult with your supplier and a building inspector for the correct mix. Typically, a yard of concrete calls for five 94-pound bags of Portland cement, 20 cubic feet of gravel, and 15 cubic feet of sand. Combine the ingredients using these ratios: $4\frac{1}{2}$ shovelfuls of gravel, 2 shovelfuls of cement, and $3\frac{1}{2}$ shovelfuls of sand.

With the mixer off, add several gallons of water and all the gravel. Turn the mixer on to scour the drum. Add all the sand, along with all but the last 10 percent of the water. Next, add the Portland cement. Once the mixture is a uniform color and texture, add the air-entraining agent if you're using it. Continue mixing for a couple of minutes more, adding more water until you achieve the right consistency.

ORDERING READY-MIX

Many ready-mix companies do not want to bother with any quantity less than a yard. Others have special trucks designed to mix smaller amounts at the job site. If one company does not want your business, call other companies until you find one that does.

Make sure that the concrete meets or exceeds code requirements, which may specify number of sacks of cement per yard, slump

(see page 104), p.s.i. (pounds per square inch) rating, and perhaps additives. Check that your concrete will be delivered "fresh"; if yours is the second or third stop on a truck's route, the concrete will be old and could set up quickly.

THE RIGHT CONSISTENCY

Properly mixed concrete is completely wet, so it does not crumble; but it is not soupy. If (wearing gloves) you pick some up and squeeze, it should roughly hold its shape, and liquid should not drip through your fingers.

Another way to test for consistency: Drop a shovelful on a flat surface and slice through it with the shovel blade. It should hold its basic shape, yet be liquid enough to pour.

pouring a concrete slab

This is an ambitious undertaking; the larger the slab, the more ambitious the effort. If possible, begin with a small project— say, a slab 60 square feet or smaller. The work is physically demanding, and all the operations must be performed in a timely manner, before the concrete hardens. See pages 104–7 for calculating and mixing or ordering concrete.

PLANNING THE FINISH

A broom finish is a good idea for many outdoor slabs because the rough surface provides traction; the concrete won't be slippery when it rains. If you choose a broom finish, spend some time practicing: Make a 4 × 6-foot frame from 2 × 4s and attach it to a piece of plywood. Mix a 60-pound bag of concrete and pour it into the frame. Screed and finish the concrete as described on pages 113–15.

Very smooth finishes are best reserved for indoor slabs, such as garage and basement floors. If you want a very smooth surface, hire a professional finisher. It takes a good deal of practice to learn how to produce a steel-trowel finish.

HOW IT'S PUT TOGETHER

To remain free of cracks, concrete slab must rest on a stable subsurface—typically, a 4- or 5-inch-thick layer of compactible gravel that has been compressed with a vibrating plate compactor (see page 62). The concrete itself should meet local codes for strength and should be at least 3 inches thick for a patio or walkway and at least 4 inches thick for a driveway. To contain future cracking, the concrete should be reinforced with 6-inch wire mesh (as shown). Consider adding fiber mesh to prevent cracking during the cure.

In areas with freezing winters, a slab will "float," that is, rise and fall slightly when the ground freezes and thaws. Also, a slab may settle slightly. To prevent the cracks that would result, a fibrous isolation joint separates the slab from the house or any other

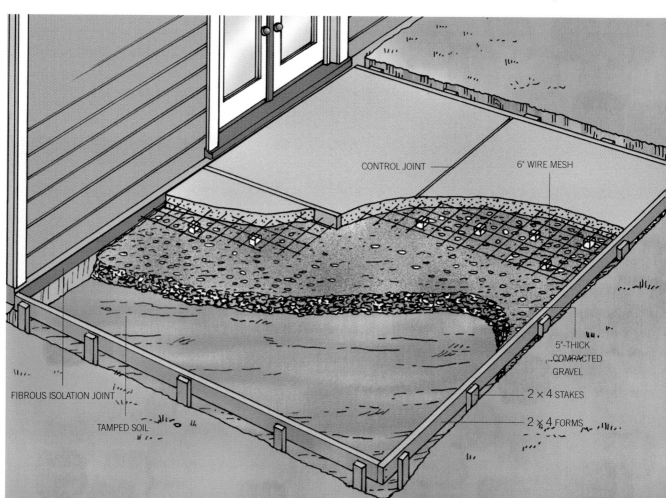

CONTROL JOINT

6" WIRE MESH

5"-THICK COMPACTED GRAVEL

2 × 4 STAKES

2 × 4 FORMS

FIBROUS ISOLATION JOINT

TAMPED SOIL

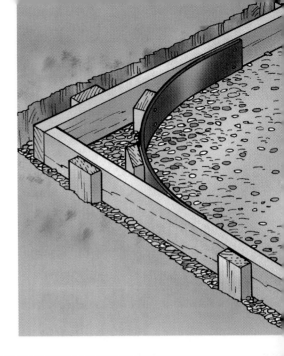

abutting structure. No matter what you do, any concrete slab will experience some cracking. To contain the cracks, control joints (see step 10, page 115) are spaced every 6 to 8 feet. Use an edging tool to round off all exposed edges, which will prevent chipping.

BUILDING FORMS

Lay out the site and remove any sod (see pages 58–61). Use 2 × 4s to build the form if you want a 3 ½- or 4-inch-thick slab; use 2 × 6s for a thicker slab. Build the forms as you would construct wood edging (see pages 66–67). However, if the forms will be removed after the concrete is poured, anchor the stakes to the forms by driving screws or double-headed nails from the outside rather than from the inside of the form. Forms perpendicular to the house should slope down and away from the house at a rate of about ¼ inch per foot. Forms that are parallel to the house should be level.

Forms should be firmly anchored with stakes every few feet. The form boards should feel solid when you kick them outward from the inside of the slab area. The illustration at top right shows a good way to firmly anchor a curved section.

Stretch a grid of string lines and excavate the area, following the directions on pages 62–63. Think through how you will screed the concrete (page 113); for instance, will it be possible for a person to kneel on either side when screeding? If the slab is wider than 8 feet, install a temporary 2 × 4 screed guide.

If the edge of the slab will be exposed, brush the inside faces of the forms with motor oil or form-release oil. This will prevent concrete from sticking to the wood and will create a better-looking edge.

WOOD DIVIDERS

Building a grid of permanent wood dividers adds visual interest and also allows you to work in small sections; you may choose to mix concrete yourself in small batches rather than have it delivered. Plan a grid of consistently sized sections. Use pressure-treated lumber or the dark heartwood of redwood.

Construct the outside frame as you would standard forms. Cut and install the interior 2 x 4s and check for square and consistent spacing. If the sections are larger than 3 feet square, install interior 2 x 4 stakes, as shown, with their tops 1 ½ inches below the tops of the forms. Every two feet or so, drive 3-inch deck screws, as shown, to firmly anchor the concrete to the boards. Finally, apply masking tape to the top edges of the form boards to protect them while screeding and finishing the concrete.

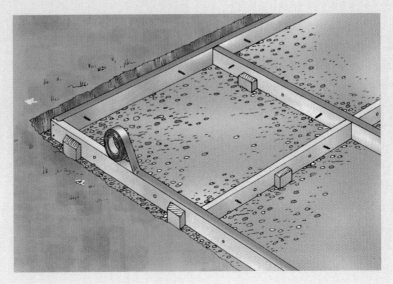

GETTING READY FOR THE POUR

Carefully plan how the concrete will be delivered into the formed area. If you are lucky, a truck may be able to pour directly into the forms; check to see if the company has chutes that are long enough. More likely, you will need to pour concrete into wheelbarrows and wheel it to the site in batches.

Pouring concrete is a messy business, so cover any nearby plants or surfaces that would be damaged by spattered concrete. Double-check that form boards are straight, are level or correctly sloped, and are firmly anchored.

1 Fill and Tamp Low Spots

Use a straight board to check the excavation for any low spots. Fill them with compactible gravel and power-tamp. Check for gaps under the form boards; concrete can seep through a space wider than $\frac{1}{2}$ inch. Fill in any space, but don't overfill; the concrete should be full thickness at the edges.

2 Install Isolation Joints

Where the slab will abut the house, snap a chalk line to indicate the height of the slab. Use construction adhesive to attach a strip of fibrous isolation joint to the house. Glue it firmly; it must stay in place when you screed and finish the concrete.

3 Lay Reinforcing Wire

To flatten a roll of reinforcing mesh, first unroll it; then roll it

backward. Use lineman's pliers to cut to fit, so that the wire comes within 1 inch of the form boards. Every few inches or so, use a metal bolster, called a chair, or a chunk of stone (not a brick, which will soak up moisture) to raise the mesh above the base. If the mesh gets pushed down while you are wheeling the concrete, you can easily pull it up to the correct height by using a rake or hoe. The mesh should end up in the middle of the concrete's thickness.

4 Make Wheelbarrow Paths

A wheelbarrow laden with concrete needs a smooth path, or it will dent the lawn and be difficult to maneuver. Lay and screw together a path made of 2 × 10s, 2 × 12s, or strips of ¾-inch plywood that are at least 12 inches wide. Load a wheelbarrow with heavy gravel or stones and test to see that you will be able to easily transport the concrete throughout the formed area. Where wheelbarrows will cross a form, place boards or blocks on either side to create a bridge. Also add short boards as needed so that the wheelbarrow never has to step up or down more than 2 inches.

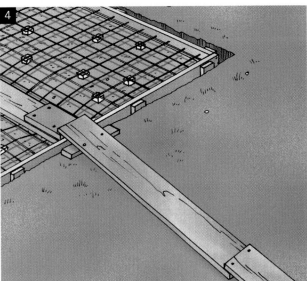

BEFORE THE TRUCK COMES

Before arranging for the concrete to be delivered, carefully read pages 112–15; you won't have time to read them once the concrete comes. If you plan to apply a custom finish, clearly understand the steps you will take (see pages 116–23). It will probably cost extra money if the truck driver has to wait more than half an hour, so plan to move the concrete quickly.

* If you want a smooth steel-trowel finish, contract an experienced concrete finisher. This is also a good idea if the slab is larger than 100 square feet, even if you plan a broom finish.

* Line up two or more reliable helpers. Trucks occasionally come early, so schedule the helpers to arrive early as well.

* Have all the tools on hand, including two heavy-duty wheelbarrows. For a large slab, use a bull float; for a smaller slab, use a darby. Also, have on hand shovels, a rake, at least one magnesium or wood float, a screed board, a jointer, an edger, a broom, a kneeling board, perhaps a steel trowel, and plastic for covering the concrete.

* Double-check that the forms are straight and firm and that the isolation joint is firmly attached. Attach any temporary screed guides.

* Test the wheelbarrow paths.

* Make sure that the wire mesh is at the correct height, or have a rake on hand so that you can pull it up at the right time.

* If you needed a permit, the inspector probably will want to inspect the forms before you pour. Also, you may need to arrange for the inspector to be on hand to test the concrete just before you pour it.

POURING AND FINISHING

Take steps to give yourself a little extra time to finish the concrete. Order a fairly stiff mix, perhaps with a slump of 3 inches or less. Stiff concrete is a little harder to pour at first, but it will actually give you more time to work the surface. (The wetter the concrete,

the longer you have to wait for the bleed water to evaporate from the surface.) If possible, have the concrete delivered on a shady day rather than on a sunny one.

It usually works best to have one person stand in the formed area with a shovel while the others deliver wheelbarrows full of concrete. The shoveler can direct traffic and distribute the concrete in preparation for screeding.

1 Load the Wheelbarrow

Set the wheelbarrow on a stable surface under the truck's chute. If possible, have the wheel resting on the beginning of the path, so that you can take off smoothly. Ask the driver to load the first wheelbarrow only half full; you can increase the loads once you get used to the work. Use a scrap of lumber to scrape the chute after it stops pouring, so that no concrete spills onto the ground.

2 Wheel and Pour

Wheel a load of concrete carefully; it's easy to spill if you have not practiced. If you start to lose control of the wheelbarrow, don't try to right it. Instead, push down on the handles with both hands. Then pick up the handles and start again. Wheel the concrete to a far corner of the formed area and pour the concrete out.

3 Fill the Forms

The shoveler should spread the concrete until it is even with, or slightly above, the top of the form boards. Fill low spots, especially against the forms, with shovelfuls of concrete. Make sure that the wire mesh is about in the middle of the concrete's thickness. Use a rake to pull it up or to push it down, as needed.

Tap the outside of the form boards, to help the concrete settle snugly against the boards.

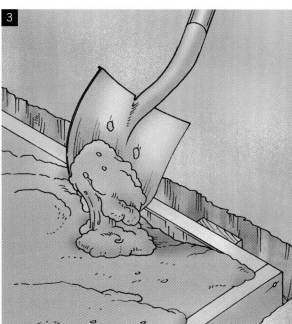

4 Screed the Concrete

Working with a helper, position a long, straight 2 × 4 screed so that the ends rest on the forms or on a form and a temporary screed guide (as shown). Using a sawing back-and-forth motion, draw the screed across the surface to flatten the concrete at the same height as the forms. If there are voids (low spots), fill them by shoveling in more concrete and screed again.

5 Remove a Temporary Screed Guide

If the slab is large enough to need a temporary screed guide, fill and screed the other section as you did the first. You may need to lay a sheet of plywood on top of the freshly poured concrete of the first section, in order to kneel and screed. When both sections are filled, remove the guide. Fill the resulting trough with shovelfuls of concrete.

6 Bull Float

Typically, you should use a bull float if the area to be floated is wider than 8 feet or so. If you have a smaller slab, see "Using a Darby" on the next page.

When using a bull float, take care not to let the leading edge dig into the concrete. Push it forward with the front edge slightly raised. Pull it back over the same territory; this will push stones down and fill in small holes. After each back-and-forth stroke, pick the float up and move it over to create a parallel stroke. Overlap the strokes slightly, so that the entire surface gets floated.

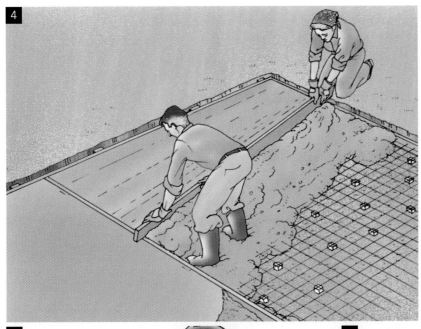

USING A DARBY

Float a small slab using a darby instead of a bull float. Hold the darby so the leading edge is slightly raised and gently run it over the surface in sweeping strokes.

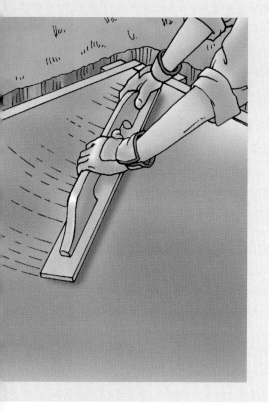

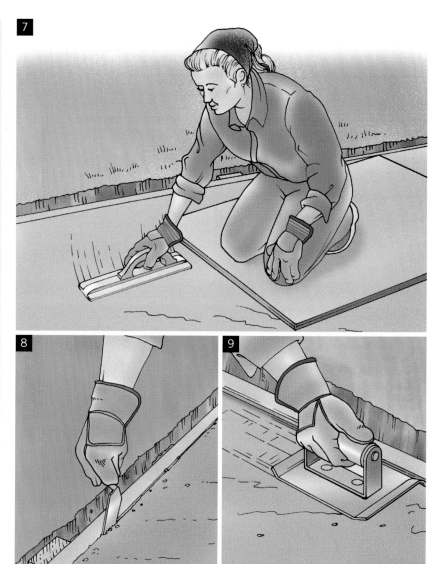

7 **Use a Magnesium or Wood Float**
Initial floating with a darby or bull float will cause "bleed water" to rise to the surface. Pay close attention to it, and as soon as the surface is nearly dry, run a magnesium or wood float over the surface. (A magnesium float is easier to use and is definitely recommended for beginners.) Hold the tool so that the leading edge is slightly raised and press down very gently as you work. If you cannot reach across a slab,

place a piece of plywood about 3 feet by 4 feet on the concrete and kneel on it; start floating at the far corner and work back, so that you do not kneel on newly floated concrete.

8 **Cut Outside Edges**
Slip a mason's trowel between the inside of the forms and the concrete and slice all along the perimeter of the slab. This will eliminate the pockets of air that can weaken the concrete. Tap the

forms with a hammer every foot or so (as you did in step 3). If you plan to give the concrete a custom finish, do so at this point.

9 **Round the Edges**
Run an edging tool along the outside edges and along both sides of any permanent wood dividers as well. The edger has a toboggan edge on each side so that you can easily run it back and forth. It will take two or three passes to create a smooth edge.

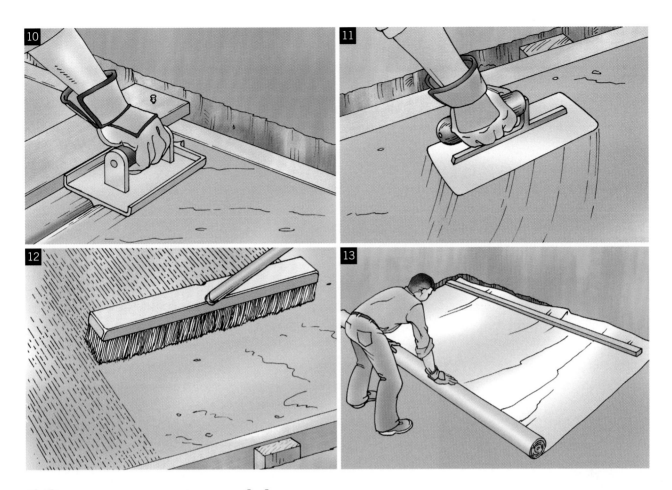

10 Make Control Joints

To prevent unsightly cracking, any section of a patio wider than 10 feet should have a control joint along the middle. Set a straight 2 × 4 on top of the concrete as a guide. Run the jointer back and forth several times until the concrete is smooth on either side of the joint. Once you have edged the corners and made control joints, use a magnesium or a wood float to smooth any indentations.

Alternatively, skip this step and finish the surface. Once the concrete has fully hardened (you don't have to wait for it to cure), cut control joints using a heavy-duty circular saw equipped with a masonry blade.

11 Trowel Finish

If you are a beginner and the surface is not quite smooth enough, go over it again with a magnesium float. How much pressure you should apply depends on how wet the concrete is. Ideally, the surface should be still wet but should not have standing bleed water.

For a smoother finish, have an experienced concrete finisher work the surface, using a steel trowel, and skip step 12.

12 Broom Finish

Gently drag a push broom across the surface. Pull it, rather than push. The stiffer the broom bristles, the more pronounced will be the texture. If the bristles are not dig-

ging in and producing the surface you like, try wetting the broom. Work carefully and aim to produce a consistent texture with straight lines. Avoid overlapping the strokes; they should be right next to each other.

13 Cure the Concrete Slowly

The more slowly concrete cures, the stronger it will be. After finishing, keep the concrete wet for at least a week. Cover the concrete with plastic or spray it with a fine mist twice a day.

After a day, carefully pry the temporary forms away from the concrete. You may be able to smooth any rough edges using an edger or a magnesium trowel.

decorative effects for new concrete

Pouring a basic concrete slab (pages 104–15) is already a challenging task. Before you decide to add an extra step to produce a decorative surface, be sure you have mastered the basics. The next four pages show three techniques that do not require a lot of skill, so they make the task only marginally more difficult.

Beyond the effects shown here, there are other finishes that can be created before concrete cures, but they require the skills of a professional. You might also consider allowing the concrete to cure and then staining or covering it with a decorative material, as shown on pages 122–31.

COLORING CONCRETE

The most reliable way to achieve consistent color is to tint the concrete while it is mixing. A ready-mix concrete company

may do this for you, or you can do it yourself if you are mixing your own concrete. Tinting the surface after the concrete has been poured produces color that is less even, but you may want a mottled or streaked effect. For either technique, the color will be more vibrant if you use white Portland cement rather than the standard gray. Unless you have a reliable recipe for coloring, practice on small sections to find a color that you like.

TINTING THE MIX A ready-mix concrete company should have provisions for adding color to the truck's mixer. Typically, they dump an entire bag of colorant into the top of the mixer; the bag dissolves in the mix. Make it clear that the

driver should not add water after you have started pouring; doing so will change the color. (Drivers sometimes add water if the concrete starts to move sluggishly.) There will likely be an extra fee for cleaning out the mixer after you are done.

To mix your own, follow the manufacturer's directions. Generally, you will mix a small bottle of liquid or powdered coloring agent with a gallon or so of water, then add the resulting mixture to two bags of ready-mix concrete. If you mix the concrete from dry ingredients yourself, take care to measure the ingredients precisely to attain consistent color.

TINTING AFTER POURING Check the package for how much powder to apply. After the initial floating, dust the surface with the powder, using your hands; let the color sift through your fingers as you scatter it. Work the surface with a magnesium float. For more consistent color, dust and float a second time.

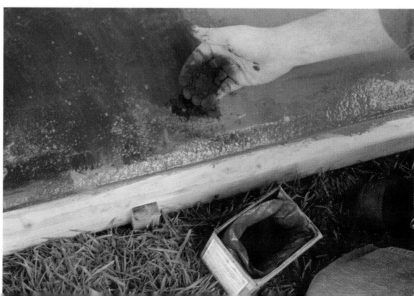

FLAGSTONE DESIGN

This decorative touch is much easier on a narrow path that you can reach across; it will be difficult if you have to lay down plywood and kneel on the concrete.

A flagstone design like this is not shown to best effect if the concrete is plain gray. Consider adding colorant to the wet concrete or acid-stain the concrete after it has cured (see pages 122– 23). You could apply stains of several colors to the various sections, to create the look of faux flagstone.

1 Tool a Pattern

For wide "joints," make a jointing tool by slightly bending a piece of ½-inch or ¾-inch copper pipe. For narrower lines, use a convex jointer made for striking joints on a brick wall. Float the surface with a bull float or a darby, edge the perimeter, and float a second time with a magnesium float. If you are skilled, you may choose to hand-trowel the surface using a steel trowel. As soon as the bleed water has disappeared, use the tool to draw a casual pattern of straight and curved lines. Aim to distribute small and large sizes throughout the slab.

2 Trowel Over the Pattern

Gently run a magnesium float over the surface to knock down most of the crumbs and any exposed gravel.

3 Brush the Surface

Use a paintbrush or a mason's brush to gently clear away any remaining crumbs and to produce a finely textured broom finish over the entire surface.

SEEDED AGGREGATE

This process takes longer than a standard broom finish, so unless you are working in a very small area, arrange for a retarder to be added to the concrete, to give you extra time to work.

Standard exposed aggregate is available in bags; colors usually run from brown to light tan. To add a bit more interest, buy smaller amounts of a colored stone and scatter sparsely throughout the surface. Buy more aggregate than you think you need; it's easy to return leftovers, but you'll really be stuck if you run short.

1 Scatter the Aggregate

Pour and screed the concrete; you do not need to float it, but make sure that all voids are filled and that the surface is flat and even. As soon as the bleed water has disappeared, use a shovel to scatter aggregate over the entire surface; aim for a single layer. You may choose to sprinkle the area with colorful stones as well and perhaps even install several decorative accent stones.

2 Embed the Aggregate

Use a flat board to gently press the stones into the concrete. Rest either end of the board on the edging, to ensure that it does not press down and create a dent. If pressing the board down with your hand does not embed the stones, walk on the board.

3 Float Over the Aggregate

If the slab is large, cover part of it with plastic to keep it wet until you reach that part. Work the surface with a magnesium float so that a thin layer of cement without any gravel in it works its way up and barely covers the aggregate stones. Avoid overworking; produce as little bleed water as possible. Use an edger to round off the perimeter.

4 Brush and Spray

When the concrete has begun to harden, spray it with a fine mist and brush away the top layer using a broom or a mason's brush. Stop once the tops of the aggregate are exposed. If stones start coming loose, wait for the concrete to harden further. After a few hours, spray with a stronger blast of water to fully expose the stones. Allow the slab to cure slowly. If a haze is present after the concrete is fully cured, wash the surface with a mild muriatic acid solution.

TRAVERTINE FINISH

This produces an effect similar to a knock-down stucco finish (see page 153). If you color the finish mixture so that it contrasts with the underlying concrete, the effect will be heightened.

Pour, screed, and float the surface with a darby or bull float followed by a magnesium or wood float. Use an edger to round off the edges. In a bucket, dry-mix one part Portland cement with 2 parts sand and add water to produce a stiff mix. When the bleed water has completely

disappeared, dip a mason's brush into the mixture and dash it all over the surface. If the mixture sinks in, wait for the concrete to become a bit harder. Produce blotches of various sizes, but aim to have an even mix of large and small blotches throughout the slab.

Wait until the mixture has started to harden—about half an hour. Gently scrape the surface with a steel trowel held nearly flat, using long, sweeping strokes. The resulting texture will be fairly smooth on the high spots and rougher in the low spots.

stamping concrete

This is the most advanced project in the book; attempt it only if you feel confident in your skills to pour and finish a basic concrete slab. It's a very good idea to hire a professional finisher who is experienced in stamping. Here we show how to stamp a modest walkway. Stamping a large patio requires a crew of skilled workers.

Stamping is generally done in conjunction with coloring. See page 116 for tips on achieving a consistent color.

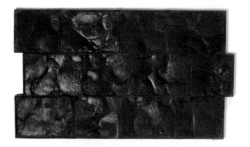

ROUNDING UP TOOLS AND MATERIALS

Supplies for this job are available at concrete supply sources, rather than home centers. Inexpensive stamps made of foam can be purchased, but they are not as reliable as the heavy-duty mats that you can rent.

Show a drawing of your job to the salesperson, to make sure that you get all the tools you need. Most mats butt against each other to create a continuous pattern, so you should have at least two or three mats. "Seamless" mats, however, can overlap and so can be used in no particular order. You may need a special flexible mat for hard-to-

reach places and perhaps a wide aluminum chisel to create lines where the mat cannot reach. Also, you can rent edging stamps, to create the look of brick edging. Be sure to get a stamping tool as well.

The same store will likely sell you the colorant and a bucket of powdered release agent. The release agent affects the color; the supplier should give you a good idea of the final appearance.

1 Apply Release Agent

Before pouring, it may help to measure and mark the forms so that you know the best place to start stamping. Pour colored concrete. Screed the concrete, float with a bull float or a darby, edge the corners, and smooth the surface with a magnesium float. As soon as the bleed water disappears, broadcast the release agent over the surface at the rate of 3 pounds per 100 square feet. This will keep the concrete from sticking to the mats.

2 Position and Stamp the Mats

Carefully align the first two or three mats so that they are precisely positioned; a slight error will be multiplied over the course of impressing additional mats. Once you are sure of the alignment, walk on the mats and use a tamping tool to press them all the way down.

3 Continue Stamping

Work rapidly so that the concrete does not have time to harden. As soon as a set of mats has been stamped, pick up each mat and lay it again. Always have at least two mats in position so that it is easy to butt new mats against them. If the concrete does start to harden, you may need to pound the mats with a rubber mallet. You may also need to touch up some joints by tapping with a chisel.

4 Pressure-Wash and Seal

Cover the concrete with plastic. After a day or two, when the concrete has started to cure, spray the surface with a pressure-washer. Use a fan nozzle held about 2 feet above the surface and move it evenly and slowly. This will remove excess release agent and will reveal darker and lighter lines that heighten the textured appearance. Replace the plastic and allow the concrete to cure for a week or so. Once the concrete is fully cured, apply acrylic sealer.

acid staining

Not to be confused with paint, which coats the surface only, acid stain penetrates beneath the surface of cured concrete for a finish that is extremely durable. Because the acid reacts with the concrete, which is itself composed of various materials, the resulting appearance is pleasantly mottled, often with marblelike veins.

This look is so attractive that many people are removing interior floor surfaces and staining the underlying concrete. Many decorative, even artistic, effects are possible using stencils, stamps, or tape to create geometric patterns. You can even stain concrete pavers. The sequence opposite shows a basic application.

Unfortunately, many people approach acid staining a bit too casually, often with disappointing results. To achieve an attractive surface, the concrete must first be cleaned thoroughly. The stain itself must be applied carefully and systematically.

If the concrete is damaged, see pages 176–79 for repairs.

Any large patches will likely turn a different hue when the stain is applied.

Choose among a large number of available colors. Be aware that over a large area, a color may look darker than it looks in a small color sample. Purchase a rinsing agent along with the stain.

CLEANING CONCRETE

Even if an old concrete surface looks uniform in color, it almost certainly needs to be cleaned. Apply commercial concrete cleaner and use a stiff-bristle brush to scrub the area thoroughly. Then rinse completely with a strong blast from a hose; better yet, use a pressure-washer equipped with a fan nozzle.

Examine the surface closely, both when it is dry and when it is wet. Any discoloration will probably be heightened rather than masked by the stain.

Remove paint by first scraping as much as possible. Then scrub with a paint remover and rinse immediately with a mild solution of tri-sodium phosphate, followed by clear water.

If you have oil stains, use a product designed to soak up the oil. Cover the area with the product, work it in with a brush, and give it time to soak up the oil. Then rinse with a pressure-washer.

Tough stains can be attacked with a solution of muriatic acid; follow the safety precautions on the label.

1 Apply the Stain

The concrete should be completely clean and dry. Wear long sleeves and heavy-duty rubber gloves. Be sure to work in a well-ventilated area, or else wear a respirator.

Fill a bucket halfway with the stain and position it so any drips can be quickly brushed; otherwise, they will show as blotches. Dip a large brush in the stain and brush it onto the concrete, using sweeping or figure-eight strokes. It is important to keep the edges wet as you work; brushing wet stain over dried stain will produce a darker color. Work methodically, so all areas receive the same amount of stain.

2 Wipe and Rinse

Have plenty of rags on hand. After several hours, dry-wipe the area to remove any residue. If a rag becomes damp with stain, flip it over or replace it, so that you are always soaking up, rather than spreading, residue. Rinse the surface with a spray of water.

3 Seal

After a day or two, apply water-based concrete sealer, using a pump sprayer, a large paintbrush, or a paint roller.

resurfacing concrete

Many companies now specialize in covering existing concrete with a polymer-reinforced product that can be colored, stamped, or tooled to produce an attractive appearance and a rock-solid surface. Unfortunately, these products are not generally available for homeowners.

However, at a home center or masonry supply source, you may find several durable concrete resurfacing products. Though only ¼ to ⅜ inch thick, the resulting surface is quite strong. These products can be colored using standard concrete colorant.

Clean the old concrete and patch any cracks (see pages 176–79). Work when the sun is not shining directly on the surface. Mix the resurfacer with water to produce a paste that is barely pourable. You will need to work fairly quickly. Spread at a uniform thickness, using a magnesium float or a broom-handled squeegee. Do not feather the edges. Instead, shape the edges

using simple forms made by butting 2 × 2s or 2 × 4s against the existing slab. Stake the forms slightly higher than the slab. Alternatively, you can simply trowel the edges square.

PAVING OVER CONCRETE

Use this technique to install paving bricks or concrete pavers. For paver pattern ideas, see page 84. You can install a permanent edging and use it as a screed guide, or install temporary 2 × 4 forms. The existing slab may have some cracks, but it should be basically stable.

1 Screed Mortar Over the Concrete The edging or forms should be higher than the slab by the thickness of a paver plus ½ inch. Make a screed out of a 2 × 4 and a piece of plywood (see page 82). The plywood should extend downward ¼ inch less than the thickness of a paver.

In a wheelbarrow or a mixing trough, combine a bag of mortar mix with a shovelful of Portland cement and mix with water to achieve a mortar that clings to a trowel (see page 140). Shovel the mortar onto the slab and smooth it with the screed guide.

2 Set the Bricks

Using scraps of $\frac{1}{2}$- or $\frac{3}{8}$-inch plywood as spacers, set the pavers in the mortar. (The pavers will settle $\frac{1}{4}$ inch or so into the mortar when you install them.) Lay a flat board on top and tap with a hammer to bed the pavers and produce a flat surface.

3 Fill Joints Using a Mortar Bag

The next day, fill a grout bag with the same type of mortar you used the day before. Squeeze the bag to squirt mortar into the joints. Keep folding the bag over as you work.

4 Tool the Joints

Once you have completed a 5-foot-square section, use a jointer to finish the joints, just as you would for a brick wall (see page 145). Tool the long joints first, then the short joints.

5 Clean the Joints

When the mortar is fairly dry, brush it lightly with a mason's brush. Take care not to brush any wet mortar, or you will smear it. Fill in any voids and holes with mortar, using a jointer or your finger to work the mortar in. After several hours, clean the surface using a mason's brush and water. After a week or so, apply acrylic sealer to the entire surface.

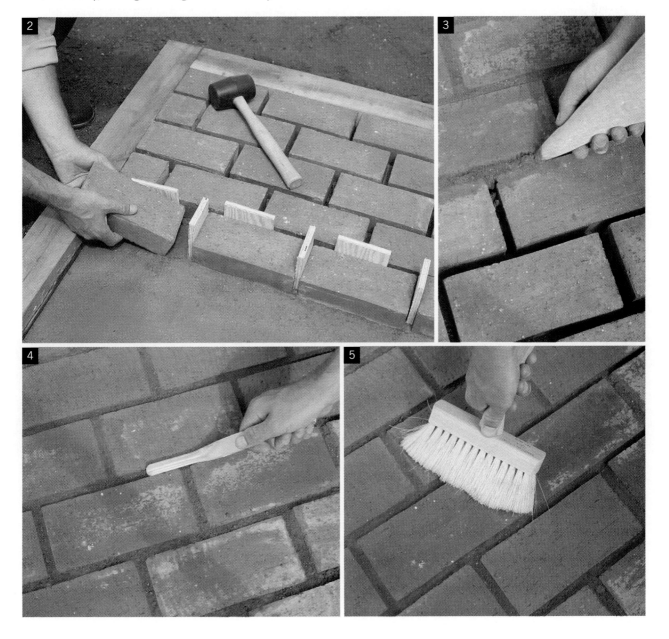

setting flagstones on concrete

You could install edging for this project, but that would mean cutting most of the stones around the perimeter; ragged edges have a natural appeal. Be sure the concrete slab is basically sound.

See page 50 for tips on buying flagstone. Sort the stones into several piles according to size. When you lay the stones out, choose some from each pile, so that you end up with an even distribution of large, medium, and small stones.

1 Apply Bonding Agent and Mix Mortar

Clean the concrete to eliminate oil residue that could inhibit bonding. Brush liquid concrete bonding agent onto the concrete, following manufacturer's instructions; usually, you need to wait for the bonding agent to dry at least partially.

In a wheelbarrow or trough, use a mason's hoe to dry-mix one shovelful of Portland cement to every three shovelfuls of masonry sand. Slowly add water and continue to mix. Achieve a mortar that is stiff enough to hold up a stone, yet wet enough to stick. It should cling for a second or two to a shovel held vertically.

2 Set a Large Stone

On a small surface, you can skip this step. To provide a reference point for height and to help ensure an even distribution of large stones, shovel out mortar and set a large, thick stone near the middle of an area that is about 6 feet square.

3 Lay Stones in a Dry Run

Fill in a 6-square-foot area with dry-laid stones. Aim for joints that are roughly uniform in width and don't let adjacent stones touch. You may need to shuffle and reorient the stones many times to get the right look. If a stone needs to be cut, hold it in place and mark it.

If your flagstone is strong and difficult to cut, let it overhang the concrete by as much as 6 inches, as long as at least two-thirds of the stone rests on the concrete. Weaker stones should overhang by no more than 3 inches. You can strengthen the overhangs by stuffing soil under them after the mortar has cured.

4 Spread Mortar

Every 10 minutes or so, remix the mortar. If it starts to stiffen, add a little more water—but do this only once. If the mortar stays stiff, throw it out and make a new batch.

Pick up one large or several small dry-laid stones and set them to the side, oriented so that you can easily recreate the planned arrangement. Shovel some mortar onto the concrete and use a trowel to roughly even it out. If a stone is thin, apply a thicker layer of mortar underneath.

5 Set the Stones

With practice, you can produce a stone surface that is reasonably level. Set the stones in mortar one at a time and check that each is close to level and about the same height as its neighbor. Make any needed adjustments immediately, before the mortar starts to set. If you feel a definite resistance when you reposition a stone, pick the stone up and reapply mortar. If a stone is low, remove it, apply more mortar, and reset it. If a stone is too high, tap it down and scrape away the excess mortar that oozes out.

6 Fill the Joints

If you want to fill the joints with mortar, carefully use a mason's trowel or a grout bag (page 125) to slip mortar into the joints. Gently scrape with a small piece of wood to provide an even fill. After the mortar has started to dry, lightly brush away crumbs.

For a more natural look, sweep in fine, crushed stone, as shown. The crushed stone will become nearly as hard as the mortar.

7 Clean the Stones

If you applied mortar to the joints, wait several hours for the mortar to harden. Then scrub the stones with water and a stiff bristle brush and a rag.

If you swept in gravel, set a garden hose nozzle to "mist" and spray the entire surface. Allow the surface to dry, then sweep in more crushed stone to fill any gaps, and mist again.

tiling over concrete

Consult with a tile dealer and choose floor tiles that are proven to survive winters in your area. Tiles with a glazed surface are slick when wet, while quarry tiles and other types have a slip-resistant surface. Installing smaller tiles results in more grout lines, which improve slip resistance. Some tiles can be cut easily with a snap tile cutter; others require a wet saw.

For a patio, you may choose to use only field tiles, which have unfinished edges; the edges will not be very visible. On a stairway or other area where edges are on display, use bullnose tiles, which have one edge that is rounded off and finished.

The concrete itself should be solid; tiling will not add appreciable strength. Chip away any high spots and patch any large depressions (see pages 176–77). Small cracks will be filled when you apply thinset mortar.

1 Lay Out a Dry Run

Set the tiles out as they will appear in the finished job. Use plastic spacers to maintain consistent joints. See that all the joints—including any joints between horizontal and vertical tiles—are the same width. Cut tiles as needed.

2 Trowel Thinset Mortar

Purchase latex- or polymer-reinforced thinset mortar. The thinset should be just stiff enough to hold the ridge shapes created by troweling. If it starts to harden, throw it out and mix a new batch. Apply the mortar using a square-notched trowel of the size recommended for your tile. First press the mortar into the concrete, allowing the notches to scrape the concrete. Then pass over the surface with less pressure, to create a flat, even surface.

3 Set the Tiles

Install any vertical tiles first. Support them with plastic spacers or folded pieces of cardboard to keep them from sliding down. Then install any bullnose pieces. To create a consistent grout line under the bullnose pieces, you may need to adjust the vertical tiles or raise the height of some bullnose tiles by adding extra mortar.

Press each tile into the mortar with a slight twist; avoid sliding a tile more than $\frac{1}{2}$ inch. Install spacers as you lay the tiles. Tap with a beater block—a piece of straight 2 × 6—to achieve an even surface. Every few minutes, pick up a tile and look at the back; if less than three-quarters of the surface has bonded with the thin-set, butter the back of the tiles with a thin layer of thinset to ensure good adhesion.

4 Grout and Clean

Allow the tiles to set at least overnight, until the thinset is not only hard but has changed to a lighter color, indicating that it is mostly cured. Mix a batch of latex-reinforced grout. Holding a laminated grout float nearly flat, use diagonal strokes in at least two directions to press the grout firmly into the joints. Then tilt the float up and scrape away most of the excess; work diagonally, so that you don't dig the tool into a joint.

Use a large sponge or rag to gently wipe the surface of the tile and tool the joints. Rinse the sponge with clean water every 10 minutes or so. Aim for joints that are smooth and at a consistent height. Take the time to eyeball and smooth every joint. Allow the grout to harden, then wipe once or twice again with a damp sponge. Finally, buff the surface with a dry rag.

INSTALLING TILES IN A GRID

If your tiles are slightly irregular in shape, plastic spacers will not work. Instead, use a tape measure and a chalk line to divide the surface into a grid of squares that hold a defined number of tiles and grout joints. Trowel thinset into a square, set the tiles, and adjust them to achieve grout joints that are reasonably consistent.

pebble mosaics

Simple pebbles can be assembled in complex patterns that resemble a tapestry or an Oriental carpet. The work is slow but can be performed in stages, making it an excellent project to undertake over several weekends. It's a good idea to start small; perhaps make some steppingstones or cover the landing at the bottom of a stairway.

The base on which you will spread the mortar must be firm. An existing concrete slab makes an excellent substrate. If you live in an area where the ground does not freeze, you can install pebbles in mortar on a 3- or 4-inch-thick bed of gravel that has been compacted with a vibrating plate compactor.

CHOOSING PEBBLES

Most pebbles change dramatically in appearance when they are wet. Choose an assortment of pebbles that will look good whether they are wet or dry.

A building supply source will have inexpensive pebbles, sometimes called drain rock. These are varied in color, so you can buy a large quantity and then sort them. You may be allowed to sort before you buy. Pebbles are often plentiful along rivers or in many fields. Because they are small, there is usually no problem if you harvest them from public land.

Choose pebbles that can present a fairly flat face when laid in mortar. It helps to have a variety of sizes. You may want some accent stones as large as a foot in diameter, many pebbles that are 1 to 3 inches, and some very small stones for filler.

Sort the stones according to color and keep them in buckets or in trays, so that you can easily access them. Lay some pebbles out on a flat surface to get an idea of how many of each color

you will need. Make a scale drawing on graph paper to visualize the project.

Build permanent edging or temporary forms, either level or correctly sloped for drainage (see pages 66–69).

1 Set Pebbles

To anchor the pattern and to keep from getting off track, dry-lay any larger accent stones that can be used as reference points. Also, it's a good idea to set the thickest stones first; thinner stones can then be set in thicker mortar. Mix a small batch of mortar, shovel it into an area a few feet square, and roughly spread it to the desired height; it should be at least 1 inch thick and at a level that is about $\frac{1}{2}$ inch below the top of the forms.

Push each stone into the mortar so that at least two-thirds of the stone is embedded. As you work, you may have to add mortar or shove mortar to the side, to maintain a fairly consistent height.

2 Fill In with Small Gravel

Keep a container of small gravel on hand and sprinkle the gravel into gaps whenever needed. Push down gently with your fingers to embed the little stones. However, it's all right if some of them do not get embedded; they can be swept away later. These small stones should be below the height of the larger pebbles.

3 Bed and Level the Stones

Every 15 minutes or so—before the mortar hardens—lay a piece of plywood over the area that you just laid and walk on it. This will embed the stones in the mortar and will help create a relatively level surface. In general, the stones should sink slightly lower than needed for the finished appearance; some surface mortar will be washed away in the next step.

4 Clean the Stones

After bedding, spray the stones with a fine mist to remove any spattered mortar. If you need to brush the mortar, use a soft brush and work gently, so that you do not dislodge a stone.

Cover each section with plastic and keep it moist, so that the mortar can cure slowly. If at the end of the project the stones are covered with a mortar haze, clean with a mild solution of muriatic acid. If a pebble comes loose, glue it back in place using latex-reinforced thinset mortar.

demolishing and reusing old concrete

An old concrete slab that is basically stable can be stained, resurfaced, or paved over with brick, stone, tile, or decorative pebbles (see pages 122–31). If it is not in stable condition (see pages 176–77), or if you just want to get rid of it, it's time to break out the sledgehammer.

REMOVING OLD CONCRETE

Most patio or sidewalk slabs are only 2 to 3 inches thick, making them surprisingly easy to break up and haul away. A well-built patio may be 4 inches thick, and a driveway may be thicker still, requiring more perspiration to demolish but still doable for an energetic demolisher.

This is heavy physical labor, so start in an out-of-the-way corner to gauge the difficulty. You can always call in pros if the task proves too hard.

1 Break Apart the Concrete

Wear long sleeves and pants, gloves, a dust mask, and eye protection; sharp chips sometimes fly around. First, simply try whacking with a sledgehammer; the slab may break apart. If not, insert a wrecking bar, which is about 6 feet long, under the slab. You may have to dig an insertion point for the bar. Place a stone or a scrap of lumber under the bar to act as a fulcrum and pry up the concrete. Have a helper hold the concrete up while you beat it with a sledge; it will break apart with relative ease.

2 Haul It Away

If the slab is reinforced with wire mesh, you can cut the wire with lineman's pliers or another hand tool. The wire ends are sharp and rusty, so wear protective clothing and work slowly. You'll need bolt cutters to snip any rebar. Break the concrete into manageable chunks, to save your back. Haul to a dump site approved for concrete or reuse the concrete.

REUSING CONCRETE PIECES

Broken up concrete makes a surprisingly useful and pleasing landscaping material—and you can't argue with the price. To shape the chunks for your purposes, simply hit the edges with a small sledgehammer. Be sure to wear protective clothing and eyewear.

The broken edge of a concrete chunk—the part that will be most visible when the chunk is used as a wall material—reveals an attractive pattern of cement and embedded rocks of various sizes and colors. The chunks will be fairly consistent in thickness, making them easy to stack for a simple dry wall or a garden bed (see pages 158–61).

Older concrete may have attractively worn surfaces that display small stones. Lay such pieces in soil or sand for a patio or path, or use them as stepping-stones (see pages 50–53).

pouring a concrete footing

A mortared wall or other vertical structure—whether built of brick, block, or stone—must rest on a concrete footing that meets local code requirements. Otherwise, the mortared joints will almost certainly crack in a year or two. Dry-laid walls do not need a concrete footing, however.

THE RIGHT SIZE

If you have freezing winters, you may be required to install a footing that extends a prescribed distance below the frost line—the depth at which soil freezes in your area. In some locales, this may mean digging and pouring a footing that is 4 feet deep. However, if the footing will support only a modest garden wall, your inspector may allow a shallower footing that "floats," meaning that it will rise and fall slightly when the ground freezes and thaws.

At minimum, a footing should be 8 inches deep and twice as wide as the wall it will support. Its top should be slightly above grade, so that rainwater cannot puddle on top.

BUILDING THE FOOTING

If the footing will abut an existing structure, install a fibrous isolation joint (see page 110) to ensure that the new footing will not affect the existing structure if the footing rises or falls.

In the method shown on these pages, the walls of a carefully dug trench act as the form for the concrete—except at the top, where 2 × 4s are used. If your soil is crumbly or if you have difficulty digging straight down, you may

choose to line the hole with plywood to make a form that's more accurate.

1 Lay Out and Dig the Hole
Use mason's line and wood stakes to lay out the outside perimeter of the 2 × 4 frame that will go on

top (step 2). If the wall is to turn a corner, check for square. Use sand to mark for a curved footing (see page 59). Dig the hole with a square-bladed shovel. The top three inches of the hole should be 1½ inches wider in all directions than the main hole, to accommodate the frame. Use a carpenter's level to see that the sides of the hole are plumb. Scrape, rather than dig, the bottom of the excavation and remove all loose soil, so that the concrete will rest on undisturbed soil.

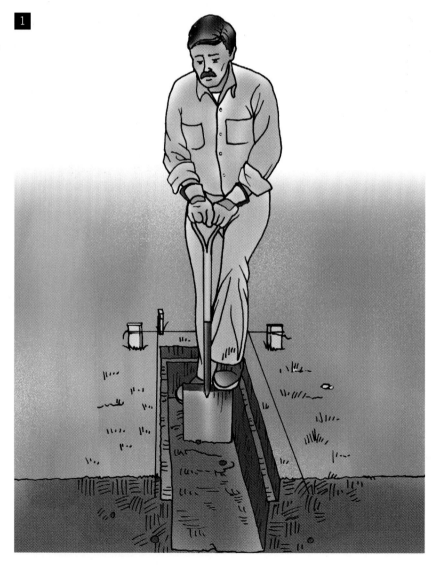

2 Frame the Footing

Cut 2 × 4s for the frame, set them in place, and screw them together at the corners. Check for square and level in all directions. Drive metal stakes to anchor the frame; using 2 × 4 stakes could cause the walls of the excavation to crumble. Drive the stakes below the top of the 2 × 4s and screw them to the 2 × 4s.

3 Install Rebar

Local building codes may call for reinforcing bar, which increases the footing's tensile strength—its resistance to lateral pressure. Typically, two horizontal pieces of ³⁄₈-inch rebar are sufficient. To suspend the rebar in the center of the footing's depth, drive pieces of rebar into the ground and attach the horizontal pieces with wire.

4 Pour and Screed

Pour concrete into the hole (see pages 104–7) and use a length of 2 × 4 to screed the top. Smooth the concrete with a magnesium or wood float.

FRAMING A STEP-DOWN

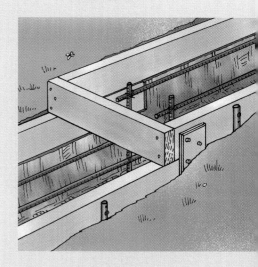

If the site is sloped, you may need to step down the footing. (Don't try to slope the footing; after all, concrete is liquid when you pour it.) Construct two frames, one for the upper level and one for the lower level, and fasten them together with pieces of plywood.

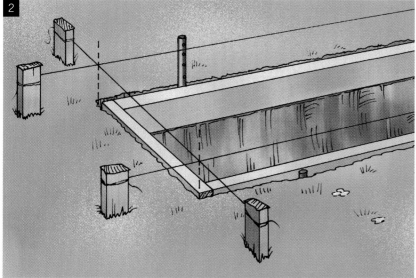

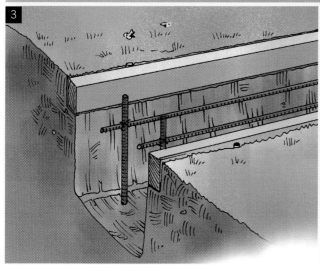

walls and structures

VERTICAL MASONRY ELEMENTS *help define outdoor spaces and give order to a landscape. They have practical benefits as well. A garden wall provides privacy and acts as a wind-break. A retaining wall stops erosion; a raised bed or planter makes it easier to garden. A wall covered with brick, stone, or stucco looks great and is virtually maintenance free. A masonry barbecue center with a concrete countertop eases outdoor food preparation.* ■ *Masonry structures that rise upward are more visible than a patio; even a low wall or garden bed can be the focal point of a yard. Though you should carefully plan walls and structures so that they will fit with their environs (see chapter one for guidance), almost any natural stone or brick structure will complement both foliage and other masonry elements.* ■ *Be aware, however, that vertical construction usually requires more skill than does laying a patio. Many brick and stone walls that look rustic and casual actually have been laid with care; a haphazard job will look sloppy rather than charming.*

retaining walls

Use a retaining wall to hold back an existing steep slope or excavate to turn a long, gentle slope into a series of terraces, each held back by a small retaining wall. The projects shown on these pages will handle most slopes. If you have a severe erosion problem—a very steep slope, or heavy rainfall that regularly washes soil away—consult with a professional landscaper.

SIMPLE STACKED STONES

A modest amount of soil can be held back by dry-stacking boulders and large rocks. Water will seep through the wall during a heavy rain. A retaining wall built by dry stacking must batter—that is, lean back toward the soil it is to retain—at a fairly steep angle. Aim for roughly 45 degrees for maximum strength.

Excavate to attain roughly the slope you want. Dig out any sod, plants, and organic matter. Lay down heavy-duty landscaping fabric and shovel a layer of rough sand or compactible gravel over the fabric. Stack the stones so that they rest on top of each other without wobbling. Fill in the spaces behind the stones with sand or gravel to improve the wall's stability. After you lay the large and medium stones, fill in any gaps with decorative gravel.

EXCAVATING FOR A RETAINING WALL

Digging can be heavy work, especially if the soil is hard or rocky. Be sure to leave room for drainage gravel, if needed.

There are three basic excavation methods. One is to cut into the entire face of the hillside at roughly the same angle as the wall will batter back. This will mean hauling away plenty of soil. The second option is to build the retaining wall at the bottom of the slope and then fill behind it with gravel and soil. This means hauling in lots of soil. The third option combines the first two, and keeps soil hauling to a minimum: Excavate the bottom half of the slope and use the excavated soil to fill in the upper half.

SURFACE-BONDED INTERLOCKING BLOCK WALL

Interlocking blocks fit together tightly to form a solid wall. Blocks like these are relatively stable when simply stacked, but the surface bonding adds strength, as well as an attractive stucco surface.

1 Lay the First Course

Pour a concrete footing (see pages 134–35) and allow it to cure. Set a row of blocks in a dry run to see where the wall will end. If the exact length of the wall is not important, plan to use all full- and half-sized blocks, so that you don't have to cut any. Snap chalk lines to indicate the perimeter of the wall.

Mix a batch of surface-bonding mortar, made for this specific purpose. Lightly wet the concrete and then spread a bed of mortar, about ½ inch thick, to cover the area where the blocks will go. Set the first course of blocks in the mortar. Use a solid-faced block wherever the block end will be exposed. As you go, use a level to check that the blocks form an even, level surface.

2 Stack the Blocks

Once the bottom course is laid, stack the next courses in a running bond pattern (see page 142). The interlocking feature will make tight corners and nestle the blocks snugly together. If required by code, fill one or more of the cores with an approved grout. Unless you

suspect a problem, there is no need to use a mason's line to check the wall for straightness and level.

3 Shim Where Needed

If a block feels a bit wobbly, stack the next course; the weight of the blocks probably will solve the

problem. If not, pick up the upper course, as well as the wobbly block. Trowel a small amount of mortar on top of the block below and set the wobbly block back into place. Tap with a hammer and a scrap of wood to settle the block at the same height as its neighbors.

4 Cap the Wall

For a square-shaped top, cap the wall with interlocking cap blocks. If these are not available, spread surface-bonding mortar on the highest course and lay solid concrete blocks in the mortar. If you want a rounded top, use the method shown on page 151.

5 Apply Surface-Bonding Mortar

Spray the wall with water to keep it moist. Mix a small batch of surface-bonding mortar and place it on a hawk. Hold the hawk against the wall as you scoop the mortar with a trowel and apply the mortar, using upward-sweeping motions. Hold the trowel nearly flat and press firmly to ensure a tight bond.

6 Smooth and Make Control Joints

Once you have covered an area about 4 feet square, use long, sweeping strokes to smooth the surface. The mortar should be about ¼ inch thick, but variations in thickness are not a problem. Rinse the trowel regularly; a clean trowel is easier to use.

To control cracking, use a concrete jointer to cut vertical control joints spaced about twice as far apart as the wall's height; for example, space them 6 feet apart for a 3-foot-high wall. Use a straight board as a guide.

7 Texture

Surface bonding mortar may set up quickly, so be ready to apply the texture of your choice. See page 153 for some options. Here, a subtly swirled texture is achieved by lightly running the trowel over the surface using sweeping motions of approximately the same radius. When applied lightly, a texture will not affect the control joints.

STANDARD CONCRETE BLOCKS

Regular concrete blocks are less expensive than interlocking blocks and thus are still a popular option. These blocks can also be simply stacked—without mortar or reinforcing bar—and then stuccoed with surface-bonding mortar. The resulting wall will not be as strong as one built with interlocking blocks (see pages 149–150), but it will certainly be strong enough for a garden wall that is no more than than 3 feet high.

1 Stack the Blocks

Pour a concrete footing, allow it to cure, and set the blocks in a dry run to determine the dimensions of the wall. Set the first course in the mortar and use a level to check that the blocks form an even and level surface.

Stack the next courses in a running-bond pattern; use a solid-faced block wherever the end is exposed. Set a block at each end and use line blocks and a mason's line to check every other course for straighness and evenness. Because these blocks are not manufactured as precisely as interlocking blocks, you will probably need to shim them with mortar from time to time (see page 149).

2 Anchor Meeting Walls

To tie together two walls when one wall continues past their intersection, chip away a channel spanning from one block to the next. Bend a piece of rebar to fit. Fill the cells with mortar and set the rebar in the mortar. Do this every other course.

3 Make a Rounded Cap

Cut and lay wire mesh over the next-to-last course or fill the cells with tightly wadded newspaper. Set the top course and then fill the cells with mortar. Allow the mortar to harden, then add more mortar and use a piece of flexible rubber to form a rounded top. (For a square top, see page 150.)

stuccoing a wall

Stucco can cover an ugly or damaged concrete, block, or brick wall and create a blank canvas that you can paint or decorate as you choose. Left blank, stucco has a soft, mellow appearance.

It will take a couple of hours to get the hang of stuccoing. Fortunately, the base coat—which you install at the beginning of your learning curve—will be covered up. Before applying the finish coat, practice on a vertical piece of plywood or on an obscure portion of the wall. That way, when you start applying the final coat to a visible area, you will have developed sufficient skill in your strokes to produce a surface that is consistent in appearance.

The masonry surface to be covered must be clean and dry, as well as free of any loose material. If a brick wall is flaking or has produced the dusty white powder called efflorescence, correct the problem before proceeding. See pages 180–81 for cleaning instructions.

1 Apply the First Coat
Paint the surface with a latex bonding agent. Pour half a bag of dry stucco base-coat mix into a wheelbarrow. Add water and mix with a mason's hoe to produce a pasty consistency. The stucco should be just firm enough to hold its shape when you pick it up with a trowel.

Place a shovelful of stucco on a hawk or a piece of plywood. Hold the hawk against the wall as you work, so that you can catch any drips. Scoop up the stucco with a straight finishing trowel and slather it onto the wall, while pressing it into place. Aim at a coat that has a uniform thickness of $\frac{3}{8}$ inch.

2 Scarify the Base Coat
When the base coat has started to stiffen, comb the surface with a scarifying tool. Work to produce indentations without raising large crumbs. For maximum strength, regularly spray with water to ensure that the base coat cures slowly—ideally, for two days.

3 Apply a Finish Coat
Mix stucco for the finish coat using the same method you used for the base coat, except make the mix slightly wetter. If you buy white stucco finish, you can mix it with dry colorant for long-lasting color. Apply the finish coat in the same way as you applied the base coat.

4 Shape a Corner

When you come to an outside corner, hold a piece of 1 × 4 against the adjoining wall as shown and apply stucco up to the 1 × 4. Texture the stucco and allow it to set partially before stuccoing the other wall.

5 Apply a Texture

To produce a bumpy surface, smooth the surface, then use a whisk broom or a mason's brush to spatter the surface with globs of stucco. You can press the globs down with a trowel, if you like.

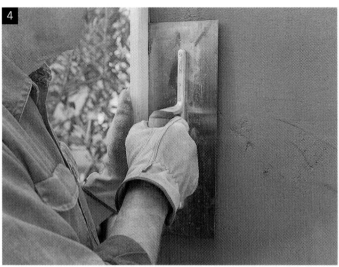

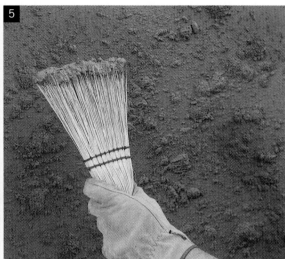

STUCCO TEXTURES

Stucco finishes are as individual as the workers who make them. Whichever technique you use, maintain a consistent pattern throughout the job. Before you can create a texture, you must first trowel on a fairly even coat of finish stucco. Any lines left by the trowel probably will not be erased when you apply the texture. Beginners may find it easier to use a pool trowel (bottom, right) rather than a rectangular trowel.

The easiest pattern is made by brushing the stucco lightly with a mason's brush. Find a pattern than comes naturally to you, so that you can easily repeat it. Rainbow-like swirls are often a good choice. Brush while the stucco is still wet. If the brush starts to leave globs, rinse it off and start again.

To make a knock-down texture, dip a mason's brush in stucco that is not too stiff and spatter the wall by shaking the brush at it. Take care not to touch the wall with the bristles. Wait about 15 minutes (depending on the humidity) and then run a trowel very lightly over the surface to flatten some of the spatters.

facing a concrete or block wall

Another way to dress up a wall is to cover it with flagstones. If possible, choose stones that are light and thin. They will be easy to cut and less likely to slide down the wall as you install them. The flatter the stones, the easier they will be to install. Use irregularly shaped stones, as shown in this project, or stones with roughly square corners for a more geometric look.

Lightweight faux-stone veneer is the easiest to install. It is thin but gives the impression of large rubble stones. Special pieces that wrap around a corner complete the illusion. Set these stones using the same methods as for flagstones.

The wall itself should be in sound condition. Clean away any oily deposits. If a brick wall is flaking or producing white powder efflorescence, correct the problem before you apply face stones (see pages 180–81).

1 Lay the Stones in a Dry Run

Lay a sheet of plywood, as wide as the wall is tall, on the ground near the wall, and place it so that you can easily pick up stones from the plywood and apply them to the wall. Lay stones on the plywood in a dry run, as they will appear on the wall. Perfect the

FACING WITH HEAVY STONES

If the stones are heavy, first install a sturdy shelf made of a staked 2 x 4 for the bottom row to rest on. Set the bottom row first and allow the mortar to harden before setting higher rows. Have on hand many short lumber scraps—1 x 4s, 1 x 2s, and shims—to use as supports. Have a helper hold a stone in place while you insert the lumber scraps to achieve the desired joint.

arrangement as you would for a flagstone patio, cutting with a hammer and chisel where necessary (see page 76).

2 Apply Mortar to the Wall

Paint a coat of latex bonding agent onto the wall. In a wheelbarrow, mix a batch of type S mortar (see page 140). The mortar should be stiff, but just wet enough to stick to the stones. Use a straight trowel to apply the mortar to the wall. Aim for a coat about ⅜ inch thick—thicker if the stones are not flat. Cover an area of about 15 square feet.

3 Set the Bottom Row of Stones

Starting at the bottom, press the stones into the mortar. Where necessary, use blocks of wood or small rocks to hold the stones in position. Make all adjustments as soon as possible. Avoid moving a stone after the mortar has begun to harden.

4 Set the Upper Stones

If the stones are light enough, continue setting stones up to the top of the wall. However, if the weight of the upper stones causes lower stones to slide down, wait for the mortar to set for the lower stones before you install the upper ones. Continue to use spacers to maintain fairly consistent joints. Every 10 minutes or so, pull a stone off the wall and check the back to make sure at least three-quarters of it is embedded in mortar. If not, back-butter stones with mortar before setting them.

5 Fill and Strike the Joints

After the mortar has hardened, go back and fill in the joints with mortar. Use a pointed trowel or a mortar bag to slip and press mortar into the joints. Wipe the edges with a damp towel, which you will need to rinse often. When the mortar starts to stiffen, strike and brush the joints.

6 Cap and Clean the Wall

At the top of the wall, install large stones that overhang the wall by an inch or more on either side. When the mortar has started to harden, wash the wall with water and a brush, and wipe the wall with a wet towel. Clean smears or any general haze on the stone with a muriatic acid solution (see page 181).

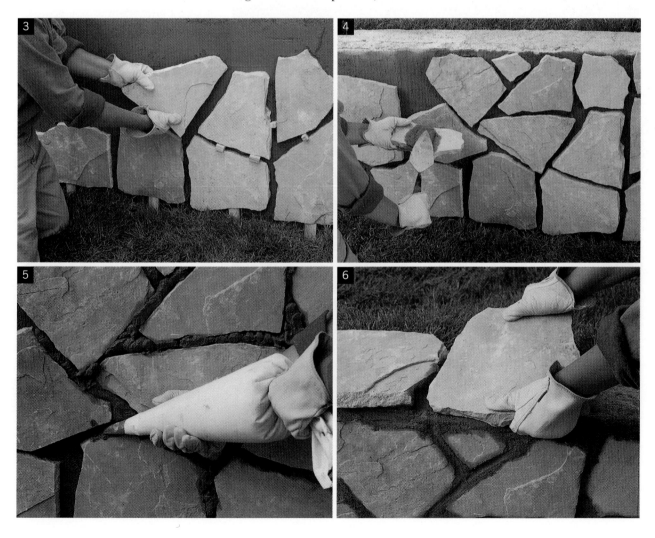

decorative block wall

Decorative concrete blocks make a screenlike wall that lets in some light. It is not feasible to cut these blocks, so plan a wall that uses all full blocks. This type of wall needs three kinds of reinforcement: Set the blocks between strong pilasters; set metal reinforcement in the mortar every other course (see page 142); and add a top cap made of pieces that span across the joints between the blocks.

1 Provide Anchoring for Pilasters
Build a form for a footing (see pages 134–35). Next to the form, set the decorative blocks in a dry run, with ³⁄₈-inch spacers to represent joints, then mark the form for the centers of all joints.

Determine where the pilasters will go and provide vertical reinforcement. Bend one or two pieces of rebar (depending on the size of the pilaster blocks) so the rebar will run up through the middle of the pilaster blocks. Pour the footing and double-check the position of the rebar.

2 Build a Pilaster
Once the concrete has cured, cut additional pieces of rebar to the height of the pilaster and tie them securely with wire to the existing rebar. Lay a bed of mortar, slip a pilaster block over the rebar, and set it in the mortar. Use a level to check for plumb in both directions. Spread a line of mortar onto the top of the block and set the next block in the mortar. Fill the cavity with mortar and keep stacking the blocks, filling them as you go. Strike the joints before the mortar hardens (see step 6).

3 Throw and Butter Mortar
Snap chalk lines on the concrete to indicate the outside edges of the decorative blocks. Spread mortar ³⁄₈ inch thick between the lines. Use a brick trowel to butter one side of a decorative block with a layer of mortar about ¹⁄₂ inch thick, then make a furrow in the center of the mortar.

4 Set the First Block

Lay a bed of mortar, ½ inch thick, on the footing. Butter one side of the first block. Lower the block onto the mortar bed, then slide it slightly to press the buttered edge against the pilaster. Check for level and alignment with the chalk lines, then scrape away the excess mortar.

5 Set the Bottom Course

Install the next blocks in the same way, buttering one side of each block. Work from both ends toward the center, keeping the blocks aligned with the joint marks. The last block in the middle is the "closure" block. Generously butter two sides of the closure block and slip it straight down into the opening. It may take several attempts before you can do this without leaving a gap.

6 Embed Reinforcement

Use mason's line and line blocks to check for alignment as you lay additional courses. Slice away excess mortar with the brick trowel and take care not to smear mortar on the blocks. Every two courses, cut ladder-type metal reinforcement to fit and gently press it into the mortar.

7 Install the Wall Cap

Once the mortar has hardened just enough to hold a thumbprint, strike the joints, using a concave striker. First, strike the horizontals, then the verticals (see page 145). Set the wall cap in a bed of mortar. Once the mortar has become stiff and crumbly, gently brush the joints.

building a stone raised bed

Raising the level of planting beds greatly reduces the potential for gardeners to develop back strain. Size the bed so that you can easily reach every corner. A bed that abuts a structure along one side probably should be no wider than 3 to 4 feet; if the bed is freestanding so that you can reach from either side, it can be 6 to 8 feet across.

This project shows how informal some masonry structures can be. Stones should be stacked fairly neatly, but the soil-filled joints are an important element of the design. Therefore, the gaps between the stones need not be consistent in width.

Soil is both a planting medium and a structural element in this project. Unless you live in an arid climate, the drainage soil—the soil that is inside the planter and lower than 8 inches from the top—should be porous enough to provide drainage after a heavy storm. The soil should also be stable; don't use organic material, such as peat moss. Try mixing two parts potting soil with one part mason's sand and one part gravel. The top 8 inches of soil, as well as the soil used to fill the joints, should be suitable for the plants you choose. Go to a nursery for advice. You may end up using more than one type of topsoil.

For instance, consider filling joints with sandy soil and planting thyme or other crevice plants that require consistent drainage.

1 Prepare the Base

Use a hose or a rope to mark the outline of the bed; there is no need to be precise. Dig a trench about 6 inches deep and wide enough to accommodate the bottom stones. Scrape, rather than dig, the bottom of the trench to leave the soil undisturbed.

2 Set the First Stones

The stones shown are "split boulders." Most of them have one rounded side and one flat side. (These are typically more expensive than regular boulders but less costly than many decorative stones.) Embed some of the larger stones in the trench, with the flat side facing up to make it easier to stack the stones that follow. To stabilize the stones, you may need to dig a shallow hole for each. Test to see if they wobble. To stabilize a stone, dig away some soil (rather than add soil). Soil that is added will likely compact over time.

3 Stack Stones and Backfill

Stack a second course of stones on top of the first. Adjust the stones so that they are fairly firm. They do not need to be rock-solid, nor do the joints need to be consistent. Fill behind the stones with the drainage soil of your choice. Fill narrow joints between stones with planting soil. Into the wider joints, insert plants and gently tamp soil around them.

4 Top Off and Garden

Continue stacking the stones and backfilling the planting area, filling the joints as you go. The top, of the bed need not be level. Fill the top 8 inches or so with planting soil and plants.

building a dry stone wall

Dry walls, composed of carefully stacked stones with little or no mortar, can be surprisingly durable. Throughout the world, many have lasted for centuries with little maintenance. The key is in the stacking. Allow yourself plenty of time to experiment with different stones and different orientations, so that each stone rests solidly in the finished wall.

A stone wall calls for plenty of heavy lifting, so work with caution. Avoid stones that weigh more than 50 pounds. Have the stones delivered as close to the site as possible, and enlist some strong-backed assistance.

It is possible to build a dry wall using roundish rubble stones, but it is very difficult. Choose stones that are at least partially squared off. You will need a large number of "tie stones" (also called "bond stones") long enough to span the thickness of the wall. Sort the stones into three or four piles according to size. Doing so will make it easier to find the stone you need. Reserve plenty of large stones to use in the wall's cap.

Make a simple batter gauge (see page 162), so that you can quickly ascertain that the sides of the wall lean inward. The bottom should be wider than the top. Based on the amount of batter and the height of the wall, calculate how wide the bottom and top of the wall will be and ensure that you have stones of the appropriate size.

1 Dig a Trench and Lay the First Stones

Remove sod and all other organic material from an area about 3 inches wider than the bottom perimeter of the wall. Scrape, rather than dig, the bottom of the excavation, so that the stones will rest on undisturbed soil. Check with a straightedge to be sure that the excavation is

3 Furrow the Mortar

Turn the trowel upside down and drag its point through the mortar to produce a channel about half the thickness of the mortar line. Take care that the mortar does not slide off the side of the bricks. If excess mortar does slide onto the bricks below, slice the mortar off in the same manner as shown in step 6.

4 Butter a Brick End

Every brick, except the first one in a course, needs to have at least one end buttered. To do so, hold the brick in one hand and load the trowel with a small amount of mortar. Scrape the trowel at a 45-degree angle to the brick end and then lightly pull the trowel back; shape the mortar in this way in all four directions.

5 Push a Brick into Place

Set the brick on the mortar bed, about 2 inches away from the brick it will abut, and slide it into place. Ideally, a little mortar will squeeze out of all the joints. Any small gaps at the joints can be filled in when you strike the joint (see step 7, page 144). If there are gaps greater than an inch, remove the brick and start again.

If a brick sits too high, tap it down, using the handle of the trowel. If it is too low, do not pull it upward; that would create a weak joint. Remove the brick, scrape off the mortar, and start again.

6 Slice Off the Excess

Use the trowel like a knife to slice off the squeezed-out mortar. If you slice quickly and in one motion, little mortar will smear onto the face of the bricks.

Every 10 minutes or so (depending on the heat and humidity), strike and perhaps clean the joints (see page 144).

brick garden walls

Garden walls are freestanding, which means that they do not retain soil. Low, short garden walls can be built with a single wythe—that is, with only one horizontal row of bricks. But such walls are not strong; you can even push them over by hand. Double-wythe brick walls are much stronger, although if they are more than 2 feet high they may not be strong enough to act as retaining walls.

Any mortared wall—brick or otherwise—must rest atop a solid concrete footing (see pages 134–35). Wait a week or so for the footing concrete to cure before building the wall. Before you start laying bricks, practice the mortar techniques shown on pages 140–41.

To quickly measure the bricks for the correct height, make a story pole. Lay a number of bricks with ⅜-inch spaces between them, on edge on a flat surface. Then lay a length of 1 × 2 or 1 × 4 next to the bricks and draw marks indicating the centers of each mortar joint. Alternatively, purchase a ready-made story pole. A standard model has marks every 8 inches to indicate three courses of common brick plus the mortar joints.

CHOOSING A BOND

For strength, a freestanding brick wall must have two wythes—essentially two parallel, abutting walls. Usually, some bricks are turned sideways to tie the wythes together; these bricks are called "headers," while the rest of the bricks are the "stretchers." Over the centuries, masons have developed patterns, called "bonds,"

that combine headers and stretchers in regular patterns.

Most bonds require cutting bricks. To help you maintain rhythm and concentration as you throw mortar and lay bricks, cut a number of bricks factory-style ahead of time. For cutting techniques, see pages 76–79.

RUNNING BOND has no headers. Be sure to embed metal reinforcement in the mortar every four or five courses to tie the wythes

together. Cut ladder-type reinforcement roughly to fit, as shown below, or push corrugated wall ties into the mortar every foot or so.

FLEMISH BOND alternates headers and stretchers in each course. You'll need to cut closure bricks at the corners.

ENGLISH BOND alternates courses of headers and stretchers. This pattern also requires you to cut closure bricks at the corners.

COMMON BOND, also known as American bond, is shown being installed on pages 143–44. It uses headers every fifth course and requires a small amount of extra cutting.

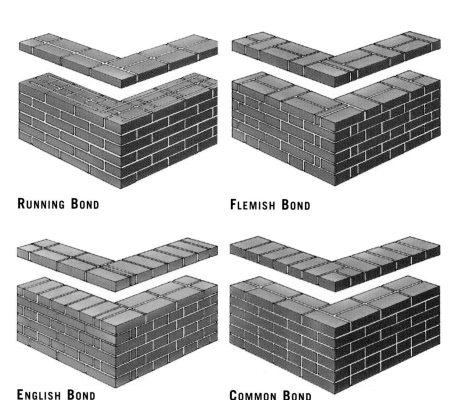

RUNNING BOND

FLEMISH BOND

ENGLISH BOND

COMMON BOND

1 Lay a Dry Run

Snap chalk lines on the footing indicating the outline of the wall. Place the bricks on the footing in a dry run, with ⅜- or ½-inch dowels between them to represent the joints. Make sure that you understand how the bricks will be laid out at the corner; you may need to cut a brick or two. You may choose to minimize cutting by adjusting the thickness of the joint or by moving one wall over an inch or two. With a pencil, mark the footing for the centers of each joint.

2 Lay the First Bricks

Remove the dry-laid bricks. Starting at a corner or at the end of a wall, throw a line of mortar for the first three bricks and butter the brick ends for all but the first brick (see pages 140–41). Push the bricks into place; see that the centers of the joints are at the pencil marks. Use a level to check that the bricks form an even surface in both directions. Scrape away excess mortar. Repeat for the second wythe and lay bricks for the start of an adjoining wall if you are at a corner.

3 Lay a Header Course

Be sure you understand how the bricks must be stacked. As you stack, every now and then hold a level against the joints, to see that they line up vertically. For common bond, a header course needs two three-quarter bricks and two one-quarter bricks, known as closures, at each corner.

Scrape away excess mortar as you go. Every so often, check the joints to see if they need to be struck; see step 7.

4 Build a Lead

Continue building the corner or the end of the wall, which is called a "lead." Make a stack seven or eight bricks high. The higher the lead, the longer it must be. As you go, use a level to check that the corner is plumb and the courses level. Use a story pole to check joint thickness. Finally, lay a straightedge diagonally on the corners to see that the bricks form regular "stair steps" at the unfinished end. Do not slide bricks to adjust their position, unless you have laid them within the past two minutes.

5 String a Line Between Leads

Build a lead at the other end of the wall in the same way as you built the first (step 4). Use the story pole to check that the bricks in one lead are the same height as the bricks in the other. Lay all the in-between bricks for the bottom course of both wythes, using the pencil lines as guides. Hook mason's blocks and stretch a mason's line from one lead to the other at the center of a joint. The line should be about ⅛ inch from the corners of the bricks. Be sure that the line is taut.

6 Fill In Between the Leads

For each course, move the line blocks up one joint and use the line as a guide for the height and for the outer edge of the wall.

Ensure that no bricks actually touch the line; that would throw them out of alignment. The last brick in the middle of a course, called the "closure brick," is buttered at both ends. Butter it generously and slip it in straight down; avoid sliding it. You may need to use a striking tool to force more mortar into one joint.

7 Strike the Joints

Every 20 minutes or so, depending on the weather conditions, test the joints by pressing with your thumb. If a thumbprint holds its shape, it's time to strike. Timing is critical; if the mortar starts to harden, striking will be difficult. Using the jointing technique of your choice (see top of next page), smooth all horizontal joints, then

smooth the verticals. If a bit of mortar oozes out the side of the jointing tool, resist the temptation to smear it while it is wet.

8 Brush and Clean

As soon as the mortar has started to harden (it will appear crumbly), brush the joints lightly with a masonry brush. If the mortar smears, stop and wait a few minutes longer.

If mortar smears onto the bricks, you may be able to wipe it off with a damp sponge, but take care not to get the joints very wet, or you will weaken them. Alternatively, wait a day and then clean with a mild muriatic acid solution (see page 181).

JOINT TYPES

Striking (also called "tooling") a joint shapes and compacts the mortar, increasing its strength and ability to shed water. If you have freezing winters, choose a joint shape that sheds water quickly, so that the ice cannot produce cracks.

EXTRUDED JOINTS are simply squeezed-out mortar that has been left alone. Though rough looking, this actually requires a good deal of skill, because the squeezed-out mortar must be fairly uniform. The joints are not watertight.

FLUSH JOINTS are produced by cutting mortar away without striking the joints. These joints are typically pitted and are suitable for dry, warm climates only.

STRUCK JOINTS are produced by scraping with a trowel tilted upward. The angle creates pleasingly dramatic shadow lines. The

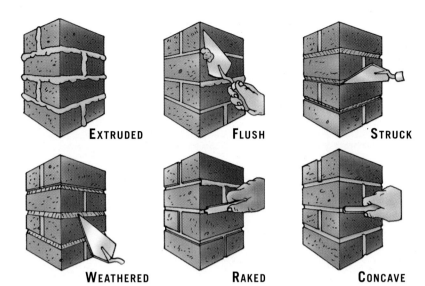

EXTRUDED   **FLUSH**   **STRUCK**

WEATHERED   **RAKED**   **CONCAVE**

joints are compacted and fairly strong, but water can easily collect at the bottom.

WEATHERED JOINTS are an upside-down struck joint. They are watertight and fairly strong.

RAKED JOINTS, produced with a joint raker, can cast interesting shadows. They are not very strong and have little resistance to water.

CONCAVE JOINTS are the most common, and for good reason. They shed water well and do

a good job of compacting the mortar. Make concave joints using a standard jointer.

CAPPING A WALL

The top, or cap, of a brick wall is important both aesthetically and practically. You could cap with a simple header course. Or install a rowlock course (bottom left), that consists of headers laid on edge. If you plan to set flower pots on top, choose something wide, like limestone block (bottom right). Set the limestone in an extra-thick bed of mortar.

a brick planter

Here we show a planter that is about 36 inches square, but you could easily make one rectangular. The planting gaps are partially filled with bricks of different colors. For a different look you could use square blocks, cut stones, or stacks of tiles mortared together—anything with the same thickness as a brick. The used common bricks shown here are pleasingly casual, and inexpensive as well.

This project calls for basic skills in throwing mortar and laying bricks (see pages 140–45). It looks rustic, and protruding plants will soon cover some of the mortar joints. But the bricks still must be straight and level or the job will look haphazard.

Make a scale drawing of the project; be sure to account for the mortar joints. In this example, the bricks are a standard $7\frac{5}{8}$ inches long, so a brick plus a joint is 8 inches long.

1 Form and Pour the Footing

The footing for an informal structure like this does not need to be massive. Dig a trench that is about a foot deep and about 8 inches wide and frame it with 1 × 3s or 1 × 4s at the top (see pages 134–35). To protect the bricks from ice, the footing should rise about an inch above grade.

2 Lay the First Course

Wait a day for the concrete to harden and partially cure. Snap chalk lines indicating the outside of the planter and check the lines for square. Set the bricks in a dry run, with $\frac{3}{8}$-inch spaces for the mortar joints; adjust the layout lines if needed. Mix and spread type S mortar (rated for ground contact) and set the first course of bricks. Use a level to make sure that the bricks form an even surface, both on top and in front.

fairly flat. If the yard is not level, you may prefer to excavate a level area, in which case the bottom course of the finished wall will appear to gradually disappear into the ground. Otherwise, follow the slope of the yard and build a wall that is slightly out of level.

Lay a tie stone at either end of the wall. Fill in with stones laid in two wythes. Fill the spaces between the wythes with tightly packed stones.

2 Lay Additional Courses

As you continue to lay stones, keep the courses fairly level. Set large stones on either side and fill in the middle with small stones where needed. To ensure a stable wall, always lay "one on top of two," rather than stacking stones of the same size directly on top of each other. Use the batter gauge to check that the wall leans slightly inward on both sides. Every third or fourth course, install tie stones every 2 or 3 feet. If you need to cut stones, see page 76.

3 Finish the Wall

Fill any gaps in the side of the wall by gently tapping in small stones; take care that you do not dislodge larger stones as you do this. Finish the top with large, flat cap stones that overhang the sides of the wall on either side. First, test whether the cap stones are fairly stable when rested on top. Then mix a batch of type N or type S mortar (see page 140) and lay a 1- to 2-inch-thick bed. Press the cap stones into the mortar.

SETTING GATE PINS

If you want to attach a gate to a stone wall that is either dry-laid or set in mortar, purchase a strap-and-pin hinge. Install the hinge pins first, then build the gate and attach the strap portions of the hinges to fit. When the stones reach the height of the lower hinge, leave a space several inches wide. Mix and spread type N or S mortar, set the pin in the mortar, and check that the pin is plumb. Allow the mortar to set before building on top of that layer. Ensure the wall end is plumb as you build it up and install the upper hinge in the same way.

mortared stone walls

A mortared stone wall must rest on a solid concrete footing; otherwise, the mortar joints will crack. See pages 134–35 for pouring a footing. Make sure that the foundation meets local codes, which take into account regional weather conditions.

Don't depend on the mortar to hold the wall together. Choose stones that are close to square and that are flat on at least some sides so that they can rest on top of each other without wobbling. Sort the stones into three or four piles according to size, to make it easier to find the stone you need. If the stones are dirty, clean them with a mason's brush and water. Use a wire brush if the dirt is stubborn; a dirty stone will not adhere well to mortar. If the stones are very porous, spray them or soak them in water just prior to installing them.

1 Make a Batter Gauge

Make a simple batter gauge with a 4-foot carpenter's level, a straight 2 × 2 or 2 × 4, a scrap of 2 × 2, and some tape. The gauge shown here will indicate a slope of about 2 inches per 4 feet when the level is held plumb.

2 Lay the First Stones on the Footing

Dry-lay the bottom stones on the footing to create an arrangement that looks good. Then move them close by, so that you can easily replace them in order. Mix a stiff batch of type N or type S mortar (see page 140). Spread a bed of mortar $\frac{1}{2}$ to 1 inch thick on the footing and set the bottom stones in it. As you work, periodically check that the mortar is sticking to the stones. If the mortar starts to harden or to crumble, throw it out and mix a new batch.

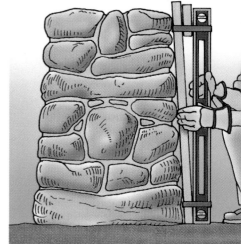

3 Lay Additional Stones

Set three or four stones in place as for a dry stone wall (see page 161). Check that they rest without wobbling and always lay one on top of two, spanning a joint below. Remove the stones, keeping track of where they belong. Spread a bed of mortar and set the stones back in position.

4 Add Filler Stones

Fill gaps larger than 2 inches with small stones rather than with mortar. If a stone sinks down too deep in the mortar or wobbles, support it in one or two places by tapping in small wooden wedges. After the mortar stiffens, pull the wedges out and stuff the holes with mortar.

5 Rake the Joints

Check the mortar periodically for stiffening. When you can press your thumb into the mortar and leave an impression without mortar sticking to your thumb, it's time to rake the joints. Hold a small scrap of wood at an angle and run it along the joint lines. This will compact the mortar as you scrape away the excess. Avoid smearing mortar onto the stones.

Work to produce joints that are consistent in depth.

6 Brush and Clean the Wall

After raking, brush the joints with a mason's brush to remove all mortar crumbs. If a stone is smeared with mortar, dampen a small towel and scrub the stone. Take care not to soak any nearby joints and rinse the towel often. Dried globs of mortar can be cleaned the next day by first chipping them with a hammer and chisel and then washing with a mild muriatic acid solution (see page 181).

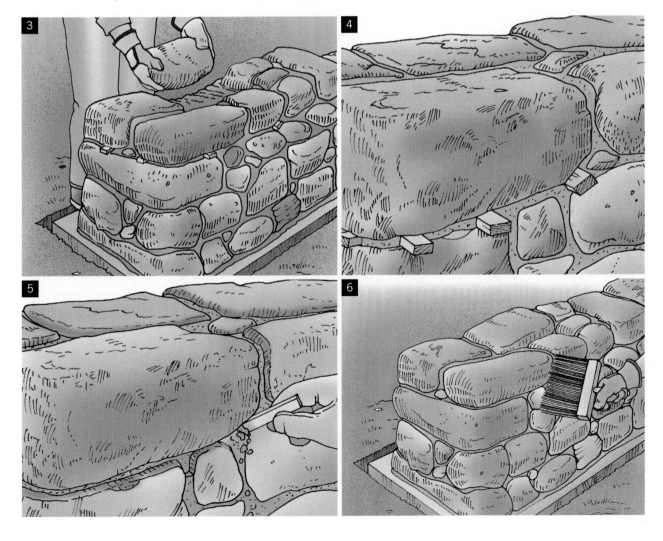

building a counter with a built-in barbecue

Outdoor cooking is more pleasant when you have counter space for food preparation—a place to set meat and ready salads and side dishes. This unit will cut down on trips to the kitchen, so barbecuing can be more of a pleasure and less of a chore. Two storage areas keep charcoal, plates, and other supplies handy and protected from the elements.

The unit shown below has a built-in charcoal barbecue. You could easily install a propane unit instead; there's room for a tank in the cabinet. A full-scale outdoor kitchen might include a sink with running water, electrical receptacles, and, perhaps, a natural-gas hookup (see Sunset's *Building Barbecues & Outdoor Kitchens* for a variety of outdoor kitchen plans).

An outdoor counter made of concrete block or other heavy materials must rest on a solid concrete footing. This project uses concrete backerboard screwed to steel studs, which is fire-resistant like concrete, but much lighter. The backerboard is covered with slate tile set in thinset mortar. The unit can rest on a patio or deck.

The framing provides openings for two doors and a barbeque unit. Metal doors made for outdoor counters are available at outdoor furniture stores.

The four pages that follow provide directions for building the cabinet, which can be covered with the countertop of your choice (see Countertop Options, page 167). Pages 168–71 show how to build a concrete countertop on top of this cabinet.

Purchase the barbecue unit and the metal doors and use the manufacturer's specs to design framing that will accommodate them.

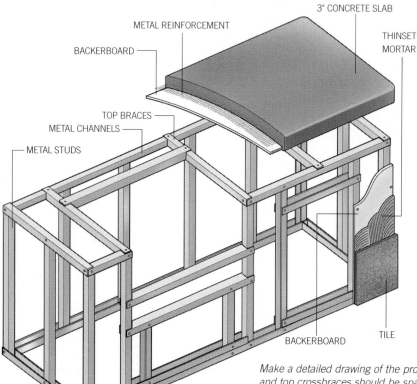

3" CONCRETE SLAB

METAL REINFORCEMENT

BACKERBOARD

THINSET MORTAR

TOP BRACES

METAL CHANNELS

METAL STUDS

BACKERBOARD

TILE

Make a detailed drawing of the project, including every framing member. Studs and top crossbraces should be spaced no wider than 16 inches apart.

1 **Measure and Cut Metal Framing**
Working with metal framing is not difficult. There are two basic components: C-shaped channels and the studs that fit into the channels. When measuring for cutting a stud, take into account the thickness of the channels—⅛ inch on either end. To make a straight cut, use tin snips to cut two sides, then bend the stud or channel back and forth several times to break it off.

2 **Build the Base**
Cut and assemble a rectangle of channels to form the bottom of the frame. For some pieces you will need to cut one or two flaps for attachment purposes; cut these using tin snips. Slip a stud into the channel and drive self-tapping screws made specifically for metal studs.

3 **Complete the Framing**
The framing will be unstable as you work; it will tie together and become solid when you attach the backerboard (step 5). As you work, check repeatedly for square, using a framing square. First frame the back and the sides. Cut the upper channels, then cut studs to fit between them. Next build framing for the front, which has three openings—two for the doors and one for the barbecue unit. To make crossbraces that support the countertop, cut studs 3 inches longer than the opening, then snip each end in two places and bend back two side tabs. This will give you three tabs that screw into the upper channel.

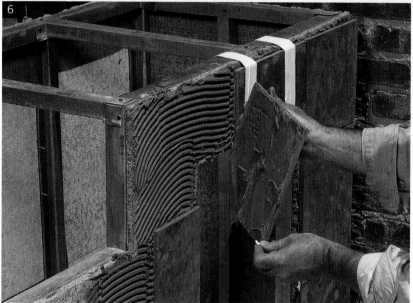

the remaining side using a knife. Before you attach the backerboard, check the framing for square. Attach by driving concrete backerboard screws every 4 inches or so into the studs and the channels. Once all the backerboard is installed, check again that the doors and the barbecue will fit.

6 Set Tiles

See pages 128–29 for general tiling instructions. Plan the tile layout, to avoid thin slivers. Note which tiles will overlap at the outside corners. Cut at least some of the tiles before you mix the mortar. Mix a batch of latex-fortified thinset mortar and apply it using a trowel with notches of the appropriate size for your type of tile. The tile salesperson should know which trowel you need. Set the tiles in the mortar, using plastic spacers to maintain consistent grout joints. Where a tile is not supported by a tile below, use pieces of tape to hold it in place until the mortar sets.

4 Test the Openings for Size

Set the doors and the barbecue unit in place, to make sure the openings are the correct size. When fitting the barbecue, take into account the thickness of the countertop you have chosen. If the openings are slightly large, you can cut backerboard to overhang the framing by as much as an inch. Taking into account the thickness of the backerboard, mortar, and tiling, determine how you will attach the doors.

5 Attach the Backerboard

When you measure concrete backerboard for cutting, subtract ¼ inch—the edges tend to be ragged. Use a drywall square or a straightedge to guide your cuts. To make a straight cut, score one side several times with a backerboard knife or a utility knife, snap the piece, and then score the opposite side. To make a cutout, use a reciprocating saw or jigsaw equipped with a rough-cutting blade to cut two sides and cut

7 Grout

Allow the mortar to cure for a day or so. Pry out the plastic spacers. Mix a batch of latex-fortified grout and apply it using a laminated grout float. First, press the grout into the joints by holding the float nearly flat and moving it in several directions. Then tilt the float up and scrape away most of the thinset. Use a damp sponge to wipe the surface and tool the joints to a consistent depth. Wipe several times, allow the grout to dry, and then buff the surface with a dry cloth.

8 Install the Doors

Cabinet doors are prehung on jambs. Set the door in place and lightly mark the area around the molding with a pencil. Lay a bead of silicone caulk inside the pencil line and set the door in place; the caulk should seal at all points. Drive screws through the holes in the jamb to secure the door to the studs on either side. Either wipe away the caulk immediately, using a rag dampened with mineral spirits, or wait for the caulk to dry and cut it away using a utility knife.

COUNTERTOP OPTIONS

Attractive options for a countertop include the following:

- Limestone slab: You can purchase several large pieces of limestone and have them cut to fit. Simply lay the limestone in a bed of mortar. Limestone is porous, so be sure to seal it regularly.
- Granite: This can also be cut to fit. It is expensive but durable and elegant.
- Tile (as shown): Install a substrate consisting of two layers of concrete backerboard. Use thinset mortar to cement the top layer to the bottom layer. Cut pieces of tile to fit, so that the top pieces overlap the edge pieces slightly, and set them in thinset mortar.

concrete countertop

Concrete countertops have almost limitless design possibilities; they have become very popular in recent years. Building counters appropriate for inside the house is a specialized skill, however, and pretty challenging for beginners. Generally, the counter is poured in a carefully designed mold, set in place, and ground to a highly polished finish.

Poured-in-place countertops are easier to make but are notorious for developing cracks. To minimize cracking, take at least some of these precautions:

- Purchase high-strength concrete. If you are ordering ready-mix, get a 7-bag mix, which has extra Portland cement. If you will use dry-mix bags, purchase "high early" concrete.
- Make a very stiff mix. Add only as much water as is necessary; the thinner the mix, the more likely it is to crack.
- Use metal reinforcement. It will not stop tiny cracks but will keep the cracks from enlarging.
- Add fiber reinforcement, available from concrete suppliers. The fibers stop small cracks, but they make it difficult to finish the top. One solution is to add fibers to the first part of the pour.

1 Build the Frame

This countertop will overhang the counter by $1\frac{1}{2}$ inches—the thickness of a 2 × 4. However, it will not overhang the barbecue unit. Cut the 2 × 4s to fit snugly and fasten them together as you wrap them around the counter. Then cut and attach pieces of 2 × 6 for the main frame. The top of the 2 × 6 here is $2\frac{1}{2}$ inches above the backerboard; the total countertop thickness, including the thickness of the backerboard, is 3 inches. Where possible, attach framing boards with screws driven into the metal framing. Also, support the frame with temporary vertical boards and use a clamp or two to hold the frame firmly together.

2 Prepare and Seal the Frame

Cut reinforcing metal to fit so that it comes to about an inch from the perimeter of the frame. Stucco lath (as shown) is a good choice for a small structure like this. Do not oil the frame; doing so may change the concrete's color at the edges. Apply silicone caulk to seal any gaps. At the corners, apply a bead of caulk to help round the edges.

3 Mix the Concrete

Experiment with concrete colors until you achieve a mix you like. (Remember, wet concrete is darker than cured concrete.) Develop a precise recipe, using a bathroom scale or a measuring cup to ensure that you add the correct amount of colorant to each batch of concrete that you mix. Take care to make the mix as dry as possible; it should be completely wet but not pourable. You can strengthen the countertop with fiber reinforcement if you like.

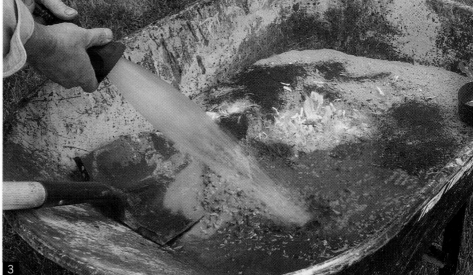

4 Pour the Concrete

Wipe the formed area with a wet rag, to ensure good adhesion to the backerboard. To minimize spatters, shovel the concrete into a bucket, then pour from the bucket into the form. Pour the first batch into the center of the formed area.

5 Add Reinforcement

Use a board or a float to move and spread the concrete so that it is about half as thick as the

countertop will be. Set the reinforcing metal on top of the concrete, and add more concrete. Spread the concrete, pushing downward to prevent voids and bubbles. If the forms bulge, pull them in straight with bar clamps set across the forms.

Continue filling and spreading concrete. Push the concrete firmly against the form at the perimeter. First, spread the concrete with a magnesium or wood float, then use a piece of 2 × 4 to screed the top so that it is level with the tops of the form boards.

6 Tap the Sides

Lightly tap the sides of the form with a hammer, to remove small air pockets.

7 Float the Concrete

As soon as any bleed water disappears, run a magnesium float across the surface to begin smoothing. Press just hard enough to bring up a little bleed water.

8 Edge the Corners

Run a concrete edger along the perimeter two or three times until the surface is smooth. As soon as the bleed water disappears, run a magnesium trowel over the surface to further smooth it.

9 Strip the Form

When the concrete seems hard enough to hold its shape, carefully release the squeeze clamps, one at a time. If the concrete forces the form outward when you do this, tighten the clamp again and wait a few minutes. Once all the clamps are off, unscrew the form boards and gently pull them away.

10 Smooth the Edge

Use a magnesium trowel to smooth the edges of the slab. If any large gaps are present, fill them by hand and trowel it again.

11 Smooth a Corner

Use a small piece of plastic to smooth and round off the corners.

12 Finish the Top

Go over the surface with a steel trowel; a pool trowel like the one shown is easier for beginners. Avoid overworking the surface; if troweling starts to roughen rather than to smooth the surface, it is time to stop.

a carved birdbath or planter

You don't have to be Michelangelo—or even an art major—to carve a simple bowl out of a large stone. With just a few inexpensive tools, patience, and determination, you can create an unusual object of rustic beauty.

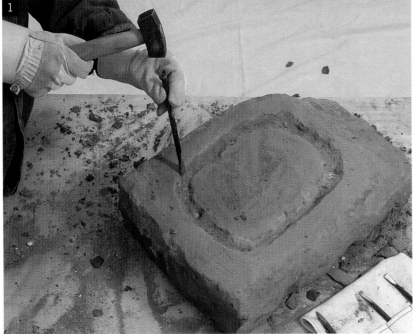

Choose a stone with an interesting shape; you will be carving only the inside, not the outside. Limestone is a common choice, since it is fairly soft. Sandstone, as shown on these pages, is even softer and easier to carve.

Stone carving chisels are not generally available at home centers but can be ordered if you search the Web for "stone carving tools." Hardened steel tools are adequate for soft stones; carbide-tipped tools are very expensive but will cut through most any stone. A modest set of chisels typically comes with a small hammer that is suited to the purpose.

Make or find a table with a soft wood or plywood surface that is at a comfortable working height. The wood will give slightly, making it less likely that you'll crack the stone as you work. Chips will fly, so wear long clothing, gloves, and protective eyewear.

1 Chisel the Perimeter

Examine the stone closely to find its grain. Carving will be easier if the grain is horizontal rather than vertical as you cut. Mark the perimeter of the bowl with a pencil. The bowl need not be the same shape as the stone. Never cut closer than 2 inches from the edge of the stone, or the edge could break off. Tap with the coarse chisel all along the cut line. Hold the chisel straight vertically until you start to chip, then bring the chisel down at a 45-degree angle.

Work toward the center of the bowl at all times. Brush away the chips every few minutes.

2 Drill a Series of Holes

You could simply continue to chip away, but you'll save time if you drill a grid of holes using a $\frac{1}{2}$-inch masonry bit. Take care that none of the holes are deeper than the bowl you want to excavate. Overheating the drill bit will cause it to dull very quickly, so work slowly. Avoid twisting or turning the direction of the drill as you work—that could cause the stone to split. And take plenty of breaks. Spraying the bit with water or oil will help keep it cool.

3 Chip Out the Bottom

Hold the chisel at a steep angle and chisel through the holes, removing chips that are no thicker than $\frac{1}{2}$ inch thick; if you hold the chisel vertically and try to dig out a thicker piece, you risk splitting the stone. To create a birdbath, chisel the bottom of the hole fairly smooth, since it will be visible. If you are making a planter, drill one or two holes all the way through, for drainage.

4 Use as a Planter

Fill the planter with soil and plants. Sandstone soaks up moisture readily, so fill it with drought-tolerant plants. Limestone is less porous and thus can hold plants that require more water.

maintenance and repair

PROPERLY INSTALLED AND SITUATED, masonry surfaces can last for centuries. However, small cracks and chips can quickly develop into large problems if left alone, jeopardizing the integrity of the structure. The sooner you stop the deterioration, the better. If water seeps into even a small opening it can slowly erode the masonry material, and if the water freezes, it can cause cracks. A couple of hours spent applying a coat of sealer or caulking a crack to prevent water damage can make all the difference. ■ Masonry surfaces in need of repair are usually easy to spot and solutions are generally straightforward. In this chapter, you'll learn how to fix common problems using tried-and-true techniques. You'll also discover some new products that will make those repairs last longer.

repairs to concrete

Before attempting a concrete repair, first determine whether the damage is structural or only cosmetic. Most structural problems cannot be easily fixed. In those cases, it is usually best to demolish the slab and start again. However, as long as a slab is basically stable, almost any damage can be corrected.

IDENTIFYING CONCRETE PROBLEMS

Concrete damage, whether structural or minor, almost always can be diagnosed by a careful examination of the surface.

- An occasional crack does not mean that structural damage exists, as long as both sides of the crack are at the same height. If a crack is ¼ inch wide or narrower, simply fill it with concrete repair caulk (see page 179). Chisel out and fill a wider crack, following the instructions below.
- A pattern of medium to large cracks throughout the slab indicates a more serious problem, especially if one side of a crack is higher than the other side. Consult with a professional; you probably need to replace the slab.

- If one section of a slab sunk lower than an adjoining section, but the slab itself has few cracks, then the slab is in good shape while the base beneath it needs to be raised. A concrete-raising contractor (check the yellow pages) may be able to raise the section up and resupport it.
- A web of hairline cracks is called "crazing." Bubblelike deterioration and/or flaking of the surface is called "spalling" (or "scaling"). Small holes scattered throughout a concrete surface are called "popouts." All three problems may be the result of poor finishing when the slab was installed. Crazing, spalling, or popouts occur only on the surface, but if left untreated can cause the top of the slab to crumble. Apply concrete sealer to keep the problem from worsening.

Better yet, resurface the concrete (see pages 124–25).

- If only a specific area is cracked or suffers from crazing or spalling, cut around the area and apply a patch (see opposite page). To repair a chipped edge or corner, see page 178.

FILLING A CRACK

Purchase patching cement that is vinyl or latex reinforced; it is well worth the small extra cost.

1 Chisel Out the Crack

Use a hammer and cold chisel to "key" a crack—chisel it at an angle, so that the bottom of the crack is wider than the top. Clean all loose material out of the crack using a wire brush.

2 Fill the Crack

Paint the crack with latex concrete-bonding agent. Mix a small batch of concrete-patching compound and use a brick trowel to stuff the patch into the crack. Then scrape the surface, so that the patch is at the same height as the slab.

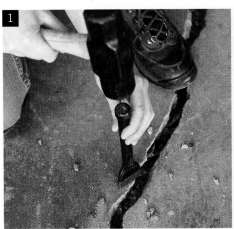

PATCHING A DAMAGED SECTION

Experiment on a scrap of plywood or in an un-obtrusive location to see how closely the color of the patch material matches the existing concrete. Allow the patch a full day to cure; it will likely get lighter in color. You may choose to add a bit of colorant to achieve a less obvious-looking patch.

1 Cut Around the Damaged Area

Draw a geometric shape around the damaged area. Using a grinder or a circular saw equipped with a masonry blade, cut the lines about ½ inch deep. Chisel out the area inside the cut lines.

2 Paint with a Bonding Agent Kit

Clean away all loose matter using a wire brush. Dampen the area and clean with a scrubbing brush. Allow to dry, then brush again. Paint the damaged area with a latex bonding agent.

3 Patch

Mix a batch of concrete patch so that it is just liquid enough to pour. Trowel the concrete into the area.

4 Smooth

Use a magnesium or wood float to smooth the surface level with the surrounding concrete, and match the finish with a broom or a steel trowel.

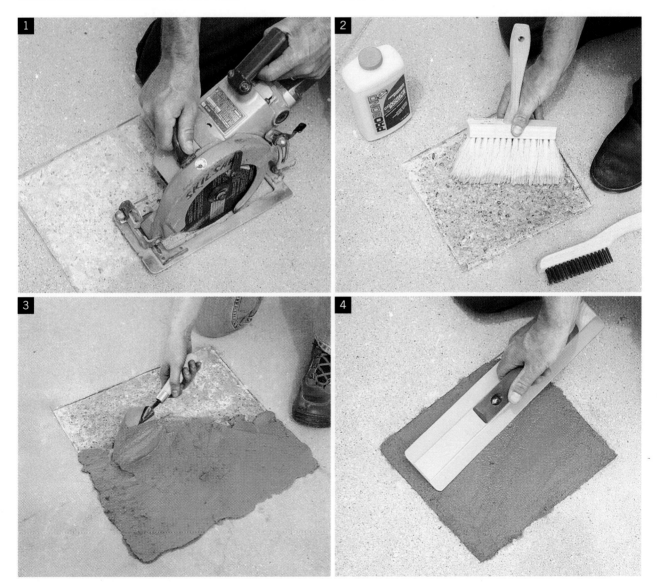

REPAIRING A CHIPPED STEP

If a corner chips in one piece, you can simply glue the piece back in place. Paint the surfaces to be joined with concrete-bonding agent, then apply a small amount of concrete patch to the stair and press the chip back into place. Use duct tape to hold the chip firm while the patch sets. Alternatively, use polyurethane glue instead of bonding agent and patch. If you don't have the broken piece, use one of the techniques given below.

1 Cut Around Corner Damage

Cut around the damaged area using a circular saw or a grinder equipped with a masonry blade. Angle the blade to "key" the cut, so that the bottom is wider than the top. Clean away all debris using a wire brush. If the damage is deeper than 3 inches, partially drive in several masonry screws (see page 184) to improve the bond.

2 Build a Form and Patch

Scrub the damaged area with a wet brush. Build a simple form using plywood or lumber that is held in place with a heavy stone or block. Spray the inside of the board with cooking oil to keep the concrete from sticking. Apply concrete-bonding agent to the area to be patched. Fill the hole with patching concrete and trowel the top surface. Remove the board as soon as the patch has started to harden and smooth again with a trowel. Then, use a mason's brush or a paintbrush to blend the patch with the surrounding concrete.

PATCHING A SMALL CORNER CHIP

If the corner damage is small, make an even simpler form using two pieces of plywood or one-by lumber and duct tape. Follow the patching instructions above.

PATCHING A LEAKY BASEMENT

If a basement wall leaks when it rains, first try directing water away from the house—check that your gutters are working properly and install downspout extensions. Make sure the ground slopes away from the house rather than toward it. If these measures do not solve the problem, and the leaks are coming from an identifiable crack, it's time to patch the crack.

Run water from a hose near the house and watch the crack to find just where the water is coming from. Turn off the water. Use a hammer and chisel or a rented electric jackhammer or chipping tool to widen the crack and "key" it. Turn the water back on. When water starts dribbling through the crack, mix hydraulic cement, made for patching basement walls, to a puttylike consistency (work quickly, you'll only have a few minutes before the cement starts to harden). Roll the cement into a

snake and push it firmly into the crack by pressing with your thumb. Start at the bottom and work your way up. If the patch succeeds, you will see the leak stop. If the leak moves higher, you may need to widen the crack there and fill it, using the same method. If the patch does not succeed, chisel it out and try again.

CONCRETE REPAIR CAULK

Caulk made specifically for repairing concrete is stronger and longer-lasting than standard caulk. It's quick and easy to apply and will seal out moisture and prevent further damage. However, this repair is not permanent and probably needs to be renewed every year or two.

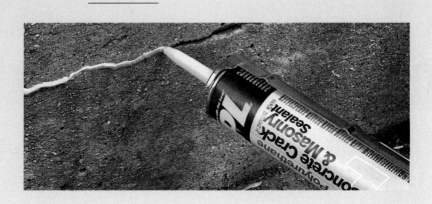

cleaning and sealing

Concrete, brick, and block are all porous, so certain types of stains can soak in where they will be difficult to clean. Prevent stains by covering masonry with a sealer. If a staining substance gets spilled, wipe it up immediately. It's a good idea to have an oil-absorbing garage floor cleaner on hand, so that you can quickly soak up oil spills.

In general, there are three escalating strategies for cleaning concrete, brick, or block: 1) Apply a detergent solution or a product made for cleaning masonry and scrub with a stiff bristle brush. Rinse well and allow it to dry; 2) If the spot or discoloration remains, try pressure-washing (see below); 3) If that does not solve the problem, try muriatic acid (see opposite page).

If the surface cannot b cleaned to your satisfaction, consider resurfacing it. To resurface a concrete slab, see pages 124–29. To resurface a masonry wall, see pages 152–55. Or paint the surface, using concrete or masonry paint.

COMMON CLEANING PROBLEMS AND SOLUTIONS

- A white powdery film called efflorescence is a common problem for brick but can also occur in block or concrete. It is caused when bricks are kept moist for prolonged periods; the water brings minerals to the surface. First, take steps to keep the surface dry, or to ensure that it can dry out quickly after a rain. Scrape and wire-brush the area, then clean with detergent or with a pressure-washer.

- Smeared mortar can sometimes be removed by scraping and wire-brushing. If the mortar is old, however, you will need to clean it with muriatic acid.

- Mortar or grout haze is a light discoloration over a large area, typically caused by insufficient wiping when the project was grouted. Try cleaning with a detergent solution first, and then with acid if needed.

- Oil stains, most common on driveways, can be persistent.

Use a wire brush carefully, especially if you are working with brick. A hand-operated wire brush can be an effective tool, but a drill equipped with a wire brush attachment is easier to use and control. Brush a small area first and check to make sure you are not producing unattractive scratches.

PRESSURE-WASHING

A rented pressure-washer offers plenty of power, but an inexpensive model purchased at a home center may supply all the pressure you need. A nozzle that directs a single stream can actually dent a brick or block surface; use a fan nozzle instead.

Use commercial concrete cleaner; it may take several applications and scrubbings.

- Paint can sometimes be removed by scraping and wire-brushing. Avoid using paint stripper—it can worsen the stain. Also, take care that you do not damage brick surfaces.
- Reddish brown iron stains can be lightened using household bleach or a solution of oxalic acid, which is often used to bleach wood.
- Ivy does not damage brick or block, so there's no harm in leaving it. If you don't like the way it looks and want to remove it, do not simply pull it off; small chunks of brick may come off as well. Instead, first cut the vine near the ground and wait a few months for the plant to dry out. Then the vines will no longer grab, so you can easily pull them away.

ACID CLEANING

Muriatic acid will not burn a hole through your hand, but it can damage clothing and cause serious discomfort if it gets on skin. Also, the fumes can make you sick. Work in a well-ventilated area. Wear long clothing and heavy-duty rubber gloves. If you are working on a slab, wear knee pads to keep your knees dry. If you do spill acid on yourself, rinse repeatedly with clean water.

Clean the surface with a pressure-washer or with a detergent solution and rinse thoroughly.

Wet the surface lightly, so that it is damp but has no puddles.

Mix a solution of 10 parts water to 1 part muriatic acid. Always add acid to the water; never add water to acid. Carefully pour or wipe the acid solution onto the surface and gently scrub with a brush. A light bubbling indicates that the acid is working. Once the bubbling has stopped, rinse the surface thoroughly.

If this mild solution does not do the trick, follow the same procedure using progressively stronger solutions—5 or even 3 parts water to 1 part acid.

SEALING MASONRY SURFACES

Wait until the concrete or mortar has fully cured—usually, a week or two—before applying sealer.

Consult with a local patio expert or a paint dealer to find the best product for your surface in your area. A basic clear acrylic sealer designed for use on masonry (rather than an all-purpose product made for either wood or masonry) is usually best.

Apply sealer using a paintbrush, a paint roller, or a pump sprayer. If the sealer soaks in immediately, another coat is needed. The second coat should stay shiny wet for at least a few seconds; if not, add a third coat.

Every year or so, test to see that the sealer is still protecting the surface. Sprinkle water on the surface. If it soaks in within 10 seconds, apply another coat of sealer.

repointing

Decades of exposure to weather will cause mortar joints to become porous. As a result, cracks and gaps appear, and these will only get worse in time. The solution is a process called "repointing," also called "tuckpointing." The old mortar is scraped away to a depth of at least ½ inch, and new mortar is applied.

Repointing a small area does not take special skill, but if you have a large area to cover consider hiring a pro. Repointers can quickly grind out joints, and they have scaffolding that enables them to easily reach second- and third-floor surfaces. They are also skilled at matching the existing mortar color.

If you're doing the work yourself, test to see that you have the right color before applying repointing mortar. A masonry supply source will have mortar samples (at left) that you can compare with existing mortar. If none of the samples quite match, consider mixing your own color, using powdered colorant. Keep track of the recipe so that you can repeat it exactly with each batch you mix.

1 Grind the Joints

If you are working in only a small area, you may want to use a hand-operated raking tool (see next step). However, this job is much easier if you use a grinder equipped with a masonry blade. Wear long clothing, gloves, and protective eyewear, because chips will fly around. Work carefully; one slip could cause you to damage a brick. Always work in a comfortable position and apply only light to moderate pressure.

2 Finish Cleaning Out the Joints

Use a hand raking tool or a

hammer and chisel to finish
cleaning out the mortar.

3 Check the Depth
The hand raking tool shown has
a built-in depth gauge. Make sure
that you have removed mortar to
a depth of at least $\frac{1}{2}$ inch at all
points. If the new mortar is too
thin, it will flake off in time.

4 Repoint
Mix a batch of type N or S mortar,
colored to match the existing mortar. The mix should be stiff, so that
it sticks to an upturned trowel (see
page 140). Work in small batches.
If the mortar starts to harden,
throw it out. Load a large dollop
of mortar onto a hawk or a large
trowel and press it against the wall,
just below a horizontal joint to be
repointed. Use a repointing tool
to scrape mortar into the joint
and press firmly to eliminate any
air bubbles. Then scrape slightly
to one side. Fill the joints slightly
thicker than you want for the final
appearance. Apply mortar to the
horizontal joints first, then scoop
mortar onto the tool and apply it
to the verticals. When applying to
a vertical joint, scrape from the
top down.

5 Strike or Brush the Joints
If the surrounding mortar joints
are neatly tooled, smooth the
joints using the striking tool of
your choice (see page 145). If
the surrounding joints bulge
outward slightly, simply brush
the new mortar to match.

anchoring to masonry

A variety of materials and techniques allow you to securely fasten brackets, ledgers, or post anchors to concrete, brick, or block. If you are sure of your layout and your measuring skills, you may choose to set an anchor while the concrete is wet. Increasingly, however, even pros are using fasteners that attach after the concrete has set, when it is more convenient and accurate to measure and install. Many of these fasteners are strong enough to satisfy building codes.

J-BOLT IN WET CONCRETE J-bolts designed to be anchored in concrete come in several lengths. The length you'll need depends on how deep the bolt must be sunk for your project—usually about 5 inches—and how much of the bolt must protrude so that the threaded part is high enough for your purposes. Use a small level to ensure that the J-bolt is plumb (as shown below, top).

ANCHORING CEMENT This is an older product that is still used because it is extremely strong. Use a masonry bit to drill holes about twice the diameter of the screws to be inserted and about ½ inch deeper than they will reach. Vacuum out the holes. Mix anchoring cement and press it into the holes. Set the anchor in place and insert the screws. Leave the assembly undisturbed for at least an hour. The cement will expand and get very hard, forming a tight bond.

MASONRY SCREWS These are not quite as strong as lag screws and shields (see opposite page), but are much easier to install. By installing more of them, you can achieve the desired strength. Some screws have Philips heads, but hex heads can be driven in more securely. When you purchase the screws, also purchase a drill bit of the correct size. Simply drill the hole ¼ inch or so deeper than the screw will reach, and drive the screw into the hole.

OTHER MASONRY FASTENERS

These products provide more ways to anchor items to brick, block, or concrete. Lag screws and shields take some time to install but are very strong. Hold the board or bracket to be anchored in place and mark for holes in the masonry surface. Remove the board or the bracket and drill holes of the correct size for the shields you will use. If the holes are large it may take time to drill, especially if you are attaching to concrete. Tap a shield into each hole, so it comes flush with the masonry surface. Set the board or bracket back in place and drive the lag screws using a ratchet and socket.

To install a sleeve anchor, drill a hole, insert the anchor, and screw

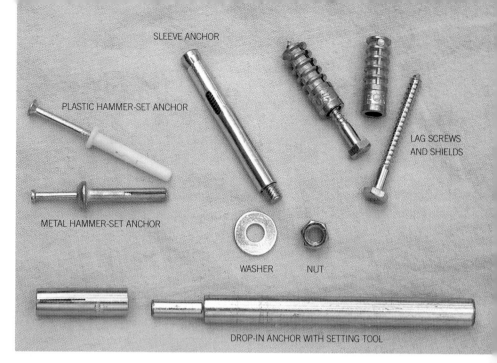

in the threaded rod. As you tighten the nut onto the rod, the anchor expands to grip the masonry.

Hammer-set anchors are the quickest to install. Drill a hole, insert the anchor, and pound the nail head with a hammer. Metal anchors are somewhat stronger

than plastic anchors.

Insert a drop-in anchor into a hole, then tap it, using a special tool (shown above) that causes it to expand and become firm. Now you can thread a bolt of any length into the anchor.

INJECTABLE EPOXY

This is a newer product that may be the strongest and easiest option. The downside is that you have to wait for a day for the epoxy to cure before fastening the anchor.

Drill holes, using a masonry bit that is slightly wider than the bolt to be anchored. Vacuum out the hole. Snip the end of the epoxy syringe and squirt epoxy into the hole. Immediately insert a threaded rod to the desired depth. Ensure that the assembly is undisturbed for a day, so that the epoxy can set rock-solid. Then, slip on a washer and tighten a nut.

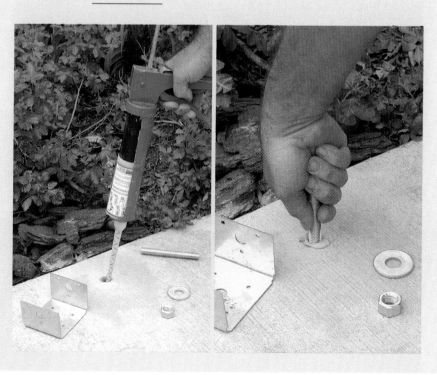

replacing bricks and blocks

If only a few bricks or blocks are damaged, they can be replaced. However, if the wall has general damage, you're better off replacing the wall or covering it with stucco (see pages 152–53).

REPLACING A BRICK

Take a brick to a masonry supply source to find replacement bricks that match in color and size. Buy mortar that matches the existing mortar (see page 182).

1 Cut Around the Brick

Use a grinder equipped with a masonry blade to cut deeply into the horizontal mortar joints above and below the brick to be removed. One slip could cause you to damage the surrounding brick, so get in a comfortable position, hold the grinder very still while you work, and press with only moderate pressure. Drill holes every two inches or so through the mortar all around the brick.

2 Chip Out the Brick

Use a small sledge or mason's hammer and a cold chisel first to break the brick and then to chip it out. Chisel out all old mortar, wire-brush away any debris, and wipe the area with a wet cloth.

3 Insert a New Brick

Wet the brick so that the mortar sticks to it. Apply a thick bed of mortar to the bottom of the opening. Butter the brick on its top and sides. Set the brick on a brick trowel and slide it straight into the opening. Scrape away squeezed-out mortar, press in additional mortar to fill any gaps, and strike the joint once the mortar has started to harden.

REPLACING A BLOCK FACE

If a block is damaged, there's usually no need to replace the entire block. Instead, chip away its face and sides and set in a new block that has been cut in half widthwise.

1 Drill Holes

Drill a series of holes around the edges and in the center of the block. While drilling, you will discover where the hollow cells are. Where you encounter the webs (solid portions running vertically along both sides and in the middle), you need drill no deeper than an inch.

2 Chip Away the Face

Cut the mortar lines around the block using a grinder or a circular saw equipped with a masonry blade. Use a hammer and chisel to break the block's face. Chip away the webs. You may be able to chip carefully and remove only half of the webs, but don't worry if an entire web crumbles. Use a circular saw equipped with a masonry blade to cut a new block in half lengthwise (see page 78).

3 Prepare the Cavity

Tap debris firmly into the holes at the bottom of the opening, so the holes are nearly filled and little mortar can seep down into them. Set two small shims, each $\frac{1}{4}$ inch thick, in the bottom of the opening. Temporarily slide the new cut block face in place, to see that it will fit. You may need to further clean out the opening.

4 Set the Block Face

Dampen the new cut block as well as the opening in the wall. Mix a batch of stiff mortar (see page 140). Spread a thick layer of mortar onto the bottom of the opening, and butter the sides of the opening. Lightly butter the bottom and sides of the new cut block, and heavily butter the top. Set the shims in the opening and tap the face into place, taking care not to push it too far. Allow the mortar to harden, and remove the shims. Fill in the resulting gaps. You may need to fill in the joints as well. Strike the joints to match the neighboring joints.

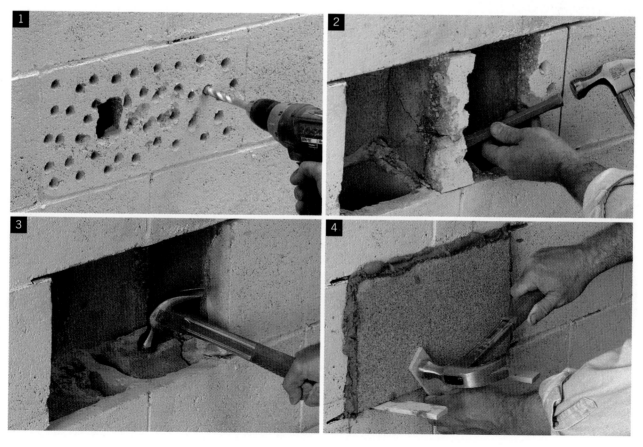

glossary

adobe: Clay bricks made into blocks. Originally, adobe was dried in the sun. Modern adobe is typically fired in a kiln and may be reinforced with asphalt.

ashlar: Stones cut into rectangular units; used for building walls with a geometric appearance.

batter: The way a retaining wall leans back toward the soil it retains, to add greater strength.

bleed water: Moisture that rises to the surface of concrete as it is being worked. Bleed water should be allowed to dry before the concrete is worked further.

bolster: A device, made of wire or of a small concrete block with wire, used to hold rebar at the correct height.

brick: A paving unit made from clay that has been molded and fired in a kiln.

buttering: Smearing mortar with a trowel onto one or more edges of a brick or other masonry unit just prior to setting it in place. Tiles may be "back buttered," meaning that mortar is troweled onto their backs.

concrete: A mixture of water, sand, gravel or crushed stone, and Portland cement.

concrete block: A wall unit formed of high-strength concrete, usually with two or three hollow cells.

concrete pavers: Paving units formed from high-strength concrete; available in a variety of sizes and shapes.

control joint: A shallow line that is meant to contain stress cracks and is scribed in a concrete slab.

course: In a masonry wall, one horizontal row.

curing: The process by which concrete or mortar achieves maximum strength in the weeks after being installed. The slower the curing process, the stronger the final product will be.

dry-mix concrete: Bags, usually 60 or 80 lb., containing all the dry ingredients of concrete; add water and mix in a wheelbarrow or trough.

edging: The process of rounding the edge of a concrete slab to make it less likely to chip when bumped.

efflorescence: A whitish discoloration on brick that typically occurs when moisture causes minerals to bleed to the surface.

finishing: The third and final step (after screeding and floating) in smoothing concrete; usually done with either a steel trowel or a broom.

floating: The intermediate stage of smoothing wet concrete (see screeding and finishing), usually using a bullfloat, a darby, or a magnesium float. Floating causes bleed water to rise to the surface.

footing: A concrete base used for the support of structures. A wall requires a long footing that is wider than the wall. To avoid frost heave in cold climates, a footing should extend below the frost line.

frost line: The maximum depth at which soil freezes during winter. This measurement is determined by local building codes.

header: A wall brick or block that is positioned perpendicular to the stretchers so that its short end, rather than its longer side, is visible when the wall is completed.

isolation joint: The junction where a concrete slab is mechanically separated from an abutting surface, usually with a fibrous isolation joint material. This inhibits cracks from forming when the slab heaves or expands and contracts differently than the abutting surface.

mortar: A mixture of Portland cement, sand, water, and sometimes lime, used to join masonry units.

paver: Any regularly sized unit used to form the finished surface of a patio. The most common pavers are paving bricks, concrete pavers, and cut stones.

plumb: The condition of being perfectly vertical, in other words, exactly 90 degrees from level.

Portland cement: A mixture of lime, silica, alumina, and iron that has been fired and then crushed into a fine powder. The result is a powerful adhesive used in mortar and concrete.

ready-mixed concrete: Concrete delivered wet in a truck, ready to pour.

reinforcing bar (rebar): Lengths of steel pole used to strengthen concrete. Rebar is typically set in the middle of the concrete's thickness, and the pieces are tied together with wire.

reinforcing wire or mesh: Steel wire welded into a grid, commonly with 6-inch squares. Stucco lath is a denser mesh that should be used for smaller projects.

repointing: Also called tuckpointing. Refinishing mortar joints that have begun to decay.

rowlock: A cap brick (used to finish the top of a wall) laid on edge and perpendicular to the wall.

sailor: On a patio, an edging brick set standing upright with its face outward.

screeding: The first step in smoothing wet concrete, typically by moving a straight board across the top form boards. Screeding also refers to smoothing a sand bed prior to installing pavers. In that case, a special screeding guide is used. The guide is composed of two pieces of lumber attached so as to screed the sand at a height that is one paver thickness below the edging. In another type of installation, lengths of pipe are used as screed guides.

soldier: An edging brick set upright with the edge facing out.

story pole: A tool used to quickly check that bricks in a wall are at the correct height. It consists of a board marked at regular intervals; each mark indicates the center of a mortar joint between bricks.

stretcher: A wall brick or block laid lengthwise. In a typical wall, most bricks or blocks are stretchers.

stucco: A particularly hard form of mortar, often made with white Portland cement, that is troweled onto a wall to form a durable exterior surface.

surface bonding agent: A stucco-like material applied to the face of concrete blocks that have been stacked, rather than mortared, in place.

tuckpointing: (See repointing.)

weep hole: A hole, near the bottom of a mortared retaining wall or a house wall, through which collected moisture can seep out. Never plug weep holes, or you could damage the wall.

wythe: In a masonry wall, the width of one brick or block board across the top form.

resource guide

Allan Block Corporation
5300 Edina Industrial Blvd., Suite 100
Edina, MN 55439
www.allanblock.com
Stackable block for retaining walls and vertical walls

Azar Mortarless Building Systems Inc.
3555 North Service Road East
Windsor, ON N8W 5R7
(519) 948-9189
www.azargroup.com
Stackable block for retaining walls and vertical walls

Barbeques Galore
10 Orchard Road, Suite 200
Lake Forest, CA 92630
(800) 752-3085
www.bbqgalore.com
Propane and charcoal barbecues

Bosch tools
www.bosch-tools.com
Power tools

Buddy Rhodes Studio
2130 Oakdale Ave.
San Francisco, CA 94124
(877) 706-5303
www.buddyrhodes.com
Information and materials for making concrete countertops

Butterfield Color
127 Gale St.
Aurora, IL 60506
(800) 282-3388
www.butterfieldcolor.com
Concrete colorants, stains, stamps

Cheng Design
2808 San Pablo Ave.
Berkeley, CA 94702
(510) 849-3272
www.chengdesign.com
Information and materials (including a kit) for making concrete countertops

Concrete Art
P.O. Box 130817
Carlsbad, CA 92013
(800) 500-9445
www.concreteart.net
Decorative scoring and staining system

Concrete Stone & Tile Corp.
23 Ridge Rd., P.O. Box 2191
Branchville, NJ 07826
(973) 948-7193
www.cstpavers.com
Retaining wall block, concrete pavers, edgings

Direct Colors
P.O. Box 1814
Shawnee, OK 74802
(877) 255-2656
www.directcolors.com
Concrete colorants

Gaye Goodman's Acid Staining
www.acidstainconcrete.com
Videos and books with detailed instructions for decorative acid staining

Haener Block
4102 Catalina Place
San Diego, CA 92107
(619) 226-8185
www.haenerblock.com
Stackable block for retaining walls and vertical walls

Quikrete Cement and Concrete Products
(800)282-5828
www.quikrete.com
Dry-mix concrete and mortar products, molds, additives, colorants

StampMaster
Creative Urethane Concepts, Inc.
907 Garland St.
Columbia, SC 29201
(803) 376-4430
(888) 901-6287
www.stampmaster.net
Concrete stamps and mats

The Stone Yard
2 Spectacle Pond Road
Littleton, MA 01460
(800) 231-2200
www.stoneyard.com
Natural and composite stone materials for walls and patios

credits

photographers

Unless otherwise credited, all photographs are by **Frank Gaglione**.

Courtesy of Allan Block Corporation: 148; Marion Brenner: 43, middle right; Karen Bussolini: 4, 6 top, 11 bottom, 13, 19 bottom, 22 top, 24 right, 85 top, 95 bottom, 145 right; Wayne Cable: 126 bottom left, 126 right, 126 top left, 127 bottom left, 127 bottom right, 127 top left, 127 top right, 129 bottom right; David Cavagnaro: 15 top, 34 top, 90 bottom left; Peter Christiansen: 28 left; Courtesy of Concrete Art: 122; Crandall & Crandall: 85, bottom; Robin B. Cushman: 33 bottom right; Janet Davis: 2 top, 21 bottom, 26 top, 92, 98 top; R. Todd Davis: 42 left, 52 top; Alan & Linda Detrick: 7 bottom, 8, 9 top, 18 bottom, 30 left, 189 bottom left; Catriona Tudor Erler: 2 bottom, 7 top, 9 bottom, 16 top, 17, 20 bottom, 24 left, 25, 26 bottom, 27, 40, 41, 90 middle left, 145 left, 160 top, 162, 172 top, 189 top right; Derek Fell: 20 top; Roger Foley: 11 top, 16 bottom, 95 top, 99 bottom; Steven Gunther: 21 top;

Saxon Holt: 43 left; Dency Kane: 6 bottom, 22 bottom; Janet Loughrey: 1; Allan Mandell: 33 top left; Jerry Pavia: 3 top, 10 bottom left, 10 top right, 12 top, 14, 19 top, 23 bottom, 29 bottom, 42 top right, 43 upper right, 75 bottom, 91 top left, 130 bottom left, 130 inset, 132 left, 133 bottom, 136, 154 top left, 158 top; Norm Plate: 168 top; Nancy Rotenberg: 15 bottom, 18 top, 102; Susan A. Roth: 42 lower right; Thomas J. Story: 44 middle, 63 bottom, 63 middle, 63 top; Tim Street-Porter/beateworks.com: 128 top; Dan Stultz: 3 bottom, 36, 43 lower right, 47 bottom right, 54 bottom, 54 top, 55 bottom right, 55 middle right, 55 top left, 55 top right, 56 bottom, 56 top left, 56 top right, 57 bottom left, 57 bottom right, 57 top left, 75 top, 107, 128 bottom left, 128 bottom right, 129 top left, 129 top right, 146 bottom, 146 top, 147 bottom left, 147 bottom right, 147 top left, 147 top right, 153 bottom right, 153 middle right, 158 bottom, 159 bottom, 159 middle, 159 top, 161 bottom right, 164, 165 bottom left, 165 bottom right, 165 top left, 166 middle left, 166 top left, 166 top right, 167 bottom right, 167 top left, 167 top right, 168

bottom, 169 bottom, 169 middle, 169 top, 170 bottom left, 170 bottom right, 170 top left, 170 top right, 171 bottom left, 171 bottom right, 171 top left, 171 top right, 172 bottom, 173 bottom, 173 middle, 173 top, 174, 178 bottom left, 178 bottom right, 178 top right, 179 bottom, 179 top, 180 left, 180 right, 181, 182 bottom left, 182 bottom right, 182 top left, 183 bottom, 183 middle, 183 top, 184 bottom left, 184 bottom right, 184 top left, 185 bottom left, 185 bottom right, 185 top, 186 bottom left, 186 bottom right, 186 top left, 187 bottom left, 187 bottom right, 187 top left, 187 top right; Virginia R. Weiler: 48; 96 top; Judy White/Gardenphotos.com: 12 bottom, 23 top, 90 bottom right

landscape designers

Clinton & Associates: 16 bottom; Cording Landscape Design: 7 bottom, 9 top, 18 bottom, 189 bottom left; Dickson De Marche: 24 right; Geoffrey Whiten: 30 left; John Newman: 48; Michael Schultz: 33 top left; Perennial Gardens Corp.: 26 top; Richard Arentz: 11 top; Yunghi Choi: 99 bottom

index